investigate
ask
tell
draw
build

THE UNIVERSITY OF
WINCHESTER

Matteo Cainer

investigate
*ask
*tell
*draw
build

3XN architects

black dog
publishing

london uk

contents

putting function in context

How a building works, or rather how users work within it, is a key measure of successful architecture. What use is a building which is convincing in other respects, but whose primary function is inadequate for purpose? On the other hand, what price do we pay if the primary purpose of the building is achieved, but in other respects it is a failure? How do architects achieve success in the round?

This book is about the working method of a successful young practice, 3XN, and their attempt to find a way of synthesising design, function and context in respect of a wide variety of building types, scales and locations. The schema of the book is itself a description of that working method: the five chapters show how 3XN investigates place; asks people about the project; tells the story of people and place in the conceptual design; draws the detail of the project; and finally builds — not just the building as object, but the building as home to a user community of one sort or another.

One might ask whether this is not the universal story of architectural practice; alas it is not, especially at a time when the curious economics of globalised development result in very poor buildings in very rich regions (like the Gulf), because there is no time for proper investigation and interaction with site, users, and even the client. Speed becomes the enemy of quality rather than a condition which can be managed confidently.

Given these circumstances, it is not uncommon for quite significant architectural projects to be commissioned from architects with scant experience of the site, and who have no dialogue with local communities or potential users. There is no design integrity other than the illusory perfection of the marketing visualisation; the result is a building whose function is masked by its iconic imagery, a quick-fire response to this month's market demands.

At the other end of the spectrum, there are architects whose expression of a philosophically rooted integrity results in an agonisingly slow working process. They become gurus for those who wish to become like them, or by others as the architects they could never be, a sort of professional conscience group. Regrettably these master architects leave the way open to the less talented to do most of the work, which may explain the sorry condition in which so many of our cities find themselves.

Happily, there are also architectural practices who think seriously about what they do and why, but have no qualms about the messy business of creating buildings in what are inevitably less than ideal circumstances. They regard compromise (or perhaps one should say constructive synthesis) as a necessary condition, not the unthinking imposition of an uninformed client or blinkered planning regime.

A characteristic of this sort of practice (3XN is one, needless to say) is the extent to which it tries to replicate that most simple of architectural relationships, where client, architect and user are as one: that is to say the creation of the architect's own house. That relationship is as close as it could be. All other commissions are successive dilutions of this relationship: the house for another individual is a modest dilution as is the building for a user-client; the building for a developer is different in kind; the building for an investor equally so; the building for the client arm of a public authority rarely pays much attention to the ultimate user. In certain circumstances, the relationship between architect and user is not only non-contractual, but utterly remote. For example, the shopping centre developer and investor have clients who are not the public, but retail tenants; the public health authority may commission buildings primarily for consultants and staff, not for patients.

What this book shows is that by developing an attitude to the process of architecture, it is possible to reverse or mitigate the dilution described above, creating the strongest possible relationship between site, client, architect and end user. This results in site-specific urbanism, where users and communities are themselves a form of site. The results are not an amalgam of the tastes and whims of the loudest voices, but the design outcome of a responsible process, in which it is more important to listen to what people say than ask them what they want. Such a process reinforces the architect's unwritten contract with the future third-party user. The most important third party of all is, of course, the public.

Paul Finch

introduction

does form really follow function ?

In recent years, with unprecedented rapidity, Danish architecture has become a visible player on the global architectural stage. One reason is that Danish architectural companies have been nurturing self-confidence and talent in their midst — talent which has matured and now reaches well beyond Denmark's own geographical, cultural and spiritual borders. Another reason is that Danish architectural companies have built up capacity and volume exceeding domestic demand. Added to which, of course, is the fact that global demand for architecture is at an all time high.

3XN has been one of the most internationally renowned and successful Danish architectural companies in recent years. They are clearly at the very forefront of the cluster of Danish architectural companies that shape the profile of present day architecture in its new global reality with its market and media focus where — under the glare and scrutiny of the global media — architects deploy their prestige and brand building architecture to growth centres the world over — primarily to the new global megalopolises — the large, and rich, urban mega centres.

If the twentieth century was the century of art, the twenty-first century with its rapid urban growth is becoming the century of the city and of architecture — at least that's how it looks so far! Here in the first decade of the twenty-first century the architect has already taken over the role of the great, classic, modern artist as the darling of the media and society's magician who creates the fix points for global investment, urban development, cultural life, mass tourism, and for the mass media in the form of television series, games and virtual worlds — the list is endless.

I can only agree with the renowned American architecture critic, Jeffrey Kipnis, that the shape of architecture on a global plane has never been better. Never before have the media focused so sharply on architecture and building construction as they do now, particularly on large and spectacular prestige projects.

The growth that drives this change — and has indeed made the change possible in the course of just a few years — is far more massive and the cause of a much more radical transformation than could be foreseen as little as just ten years ago.

Architecture and construction are not just the icing on the cake of globalisation as one might think — architecture and construction are to a great extent the very essence of what creates globalisation!

A hundred years ago 90 per cent of the world's population lived in the rural areas and the remaining 10 per cent in towns. With the present and future development over the next few decades the opposite will shortly be the case. The most common way of life for humans in the twenty-first century will — ever increasingly — be life in the colossally large conurbations that are presently emerging — from Northern Europe's Øresund Region in eastern Denmark and southern Sweden with 3.5 million inhabitants to China's gigasize municipalities such as Chongqing with its 35 million inhabitants.

This means that architecture, construction and urban planning now play much the same role as they did after World War Two in Europe. They were then — and are now — central to the design and construction of new, modern societies. Only now, this is happening at a global level and is therefore of a magnitude, scale and pace that have never been seen before in the history of mankind. The pace of development we see today is almost frightening.

A central and principally well established group of Danish architectural companies are presently consciously and strategically choosing to focus on markets outside Denmark. In the last 24 months alone Danish architects have won more than 50 international prizes and awards.

And in the course of the last five years a hitherto unseen number of non-Danish architects have been building large architectural prestige projects in Denmark. This was an extremely rare occurrence in the previous 250 years.

3XN, led by its leading creative architect, Kim Herforth Nielsen, was the first Danish company to express publicly — and not without scornful remarks from some of their colleagues — that Danish architecture and Danish architectural talent are undoubtedly benefiting hugely from globalisation, evidenced partly by the fact that non-Danish top architects now design projects in Denmark. "It benefits us because globalisation means that we face greater challenges, the fact that there are more projects out there, and because it kick starts development of our talent — in short it makes us better. That is, if we are willing to grasp the opportunity!"

And 3XN has truly grasped the opportunity and continues to do so! How does 3XN do it? And why is the company so successful? And why is it happening just now?

The reason 3XN has succeeded in the course of the last five years in creating and completing so many international projects — not only making a name for itself internationally but also contributing significantly to the general, renewed interest in Danish architecture — is because 3XN has truly understood the new reality of architecture and has taken a stance. Actually, throughout all of its existence, 3XN has always taken a stance. And still does: globalisation is not a door opening onto a meaningless black hole in an accelerating universe. Globalisation is a large window to a multitude of opportunities and potential — potential of which we had no inkling just ten years ago.

And precisely because the potential seems never ending it is not enough to have a positive and optimistic outlook. You need to know what you are about and where you want to go with your architecture — as well as with your company and the company's dedicated staff who at the end of the day

are the ones who carry the load to get the company where it wants to go. And 3XN knows this!

The company has moved through an interesting evolution in the years of its existence and has now reached the artistic and managerial maturity to be a fearless player on a global stage with endless potential. It is against this background that the company is taking an evolutionary quantum leap from its starting point, the Scandinavian tradition of functional design, which it has always respected while keeping a keen eye on new, evolving theories within architecture and urban development, starting with Venturi and Scott Brown. Today — based on its own in house developed and well managed design methods — 3XN designs bespoke, functional buildings and urban plans for every new project. These buildings and plans do not merely fulfil specifications but always exceed them adding extra value which neither architect nor client could have foreseen. Extra value which — with hindsight — nobody would have wanted to do without. The company has simply created its own special 3XN factor.

My personal guess is that the secret behind the 3XN factor — this added value that benefits everybody — is that 3XN in its design methodology, mindfully — in its own mind — has deconstructed Louis Sullivan's dictum of Modernism: form follows function.

The artistic creativity and clear talent for shape and space which informs this company's work is based — intuitively or consciously, I am not sure which, but then it doesn't matter — on the understanding of the fact that form cannot follow function until the function in question has also appeared as a potential of the form. In other words, the design work in itself creates its own meaningfulness which informs functionality. Design work — whether intuitive or systematic — does not only reveal how something might look — it also shows us how life can be lived differently — it points to the unforeseen!

In its work 3XN proves how the client, the user
or the inhabitant will derive unique value by
entering into an architectural dialogue with 3XN,
a dialogue which focuses on form as the carrier of
more than functional denotations and solutions.
Which is why the architecture currently created by
3XN is not only original and authentic — it is also
beautiful!

Because life is so much more above and beyond
functionality — beautiful, for instance.

Kent Martinussen

investigate
the site

a conversation between
Matteo Cainer and
Kim Herforth Nielsen

Matteo Cainer *As we have always discussed, this is where it all starts: the investigation of the site — and the importance of this study. This in-depth investigating is one of the elements that differentiate you from other architects and is the key to your design process. Today, architecture seems to be all about the 'signature' and the 'brand', and there is little concern or understanding of the site; the emphasis is, simply, on something that stands out. But in 3XN's work the result is of a genuine interaction with the site, and I think it is fair to say that this interaction made The Museum of Liverpool such a success.*

Kim Herforth Nielsen Well, an important aspect of 3XN's approach is that we really build on the context and the brief. We develop the existing circumstances, which results in the site being part of our conceptualisation of a project, instead of just trying to create an icon for a site. Of course, it is true, that in certain cases, it is important to create a landmark, but I think it is essential for this to be about the site. In the end, it is also a question of where, more specifically, you are placing your building — the urban context, and its social importance for the people living there.

MC *So, with the Museum of Liverpool, was it the site that most strongly influenced the design?*

KHN Well, indeed, the site's many extraordinary features played an important part, but in the end it was also the brief and the dialogues we had with the client that

We develop the existing circumstances, which results in the site being part of our conceptualisation of a project, instead of just trying to create an icon for a site.

influenced, and became the catalyst for, our design. After the client selected us for the competition, we were invited to go to Liverpool and meet with them, so as to discuss the brief in more detail. That was all in the first week — and after that we only had two weeks to come up with the final design. The whole thing was worked up in the last half of November 2004. Once we had won the competition, the project started moving at a very fast pace from the beginning of 2005, with the Museum opening in 2008.

The Museum of Liverpool acts as a bridge, literally and figuratively. The public is able to pass through its core; it physically spans the site. With its exhibitions and collections the museum also spans Liverpool's past and future and acts as a connector for its people.

✳ Museum of Liverpool

The first public twenty-first century building in Liverpool and the new British National Museum, the Museum of Liverpool, establishes a dynamic, open and accessible structure that grows out of its riverside site, responding to its context. The Museum of Liverpool is built at one of the city's most prominent development sites, which was previously used for car parking, located between the Albert Dock and the Pier Head, next to the Three Graces. The site falls within Liverpool's World Heritage Site which was inscribed by UNESCO in 2004. The building is conceived as inclined or elevated platforms, gradually forming a sculptural structure. It is fully accessible and contributes to the pedestrian flows along the waterfront. Situated next to the Pier Head, the Museum is visible from both the river and the city.

The Museum of Liverpool is one of the world's leading city history museums, showcasing social history and popular culture, and looks at Britain and the world through the eyes of Liverpool. It demonstrates Liverpool's contribution to the world, and is an engine of learning for local people and visitors

to the city. It is estimated that the new Museum will attract at least 750,000 visitors on a yearly basis, and that Liverpool, with the Museum as a symbol of Liverpool's ongoing regeneration, will be elevated into the front rank of European tourist destinations, as well as providing a brilliant place for local families to find out about their own history. The Museum is the lasting physical cultural legacy of Liverpool's Capital of Culture 2008 status.

Four main galleries; two on each of two floors, are all connected via the central atrium. They host the major part of the exhibitions and give access to over 10,000 objects from National Museums Liverpool's internationally important collections, most of which have never before been on public display. Adding to the galleries are a community theatre space for local people, drama clubs, etc.; spaces for community exhibitions, debate, performance and visual art displays; interactive learning spaces that cater for class groups or individual learners; and creative play areas for very young children and families.

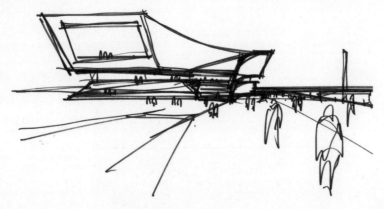

We decided that the idea
was not for the Museum
to be a part of the existing
building language, or
of the urban structure,
but rather to be part of
the promenade.

neighbours

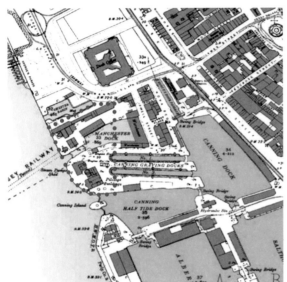

Map from 1907 and 1911 showing the Port of Liverpool Building, the open Chester Basin and the Manchester Dock. The black dotted line in the river indicates the Mersey Railway Tunnel that dates back to 1866, being the first tunnel built under the river. The design aims to integrate the history of the area.

The site (red dotted line) is situated between the River Mersey (left) and the advanced system of docks — in the bottom the Albert Dock.

With a tide of about eight to nine metres, the River Mersey is not suited for leisure activities. The hope is, however, to develop these activities and be able to connect all of the docks to one coherent system for kayaking, skating, boating, etc..

Next to the site are Liverpool's most famous buildings, the grade I and II listed buildings nick-named the Three Graces: The Royal Liver Building, 1911, The Cunard Building, 1916, and The Port of Liverpool Building, 1907. Further down the riverside is the Albert Dock that today offers entertainment such as bars and restaurants, Tate Liverpool, the Maritime Museum and the HM Customs & Excise National Museum.

MC *So, was this your first trip to Liverpool? And how did you encounter a city that had once been one of the major ports of the British Empire and a gateway between the East and West?*

KHN We hadn't been to Liverpool before. It was late November 2004, and we were completely overwhelmed by the place. Liverpool struck us as being a grand city, once a centre of commerce and one of the places from where the discovery of the modern world began. This partly explains why the buildings are so immense and varied. Liverpool had been a thriving city with one million inhabitants, however, today, the population is probably half of that. The area was added to UNESCO's list of World Cultural Heritage in 2004, and the Museum is a focal point of Liverpool's regeneration programme for when it becomes European City of Culture in 2008.

We began sketching voraciously in the first few weeks, to get a feel for the site and to try and find the best way to approach it, even though we didn't know then where the details of the scheme were going to be located. But we found that by doing this, we could understand the site and the brief much better. Of course, we'd already realised that this site was one of the most important in the city, and this excited us.

the three graces

The Cunard Building

Site

The Royal Liver Building

The Port of Liverpool Building

MC *That's very true, it being the most important site in the city. I mean, it's right beside the Three Graces, which is a fantastic focal point for Liverpool. Do you think this time around the city was looking for a more sensitive approach than previous attempts for this site?*

KHN The brief itself does suggest that, because this time it was limited only to the Museum. The whole area is very important because of these historical buildings, and it is extremely interesting to work on a site that really has its own story to tell. Pushing an idea that would respect both the place and its history was our main priority. We decided that the idea was not for the Museum to be a part of the existing building language, or of the urban structure, but rather to be part of the promenade; for the project to be seen as a piece of land art emerging from the site. We wanted to turn the area into a meeting place, where people could sit, talk and enjoy the views. It had to be a structure that blended into the area, a structure that would open up the views as opposed to obscuring or obstructing them.

juxtaposing
flow lines

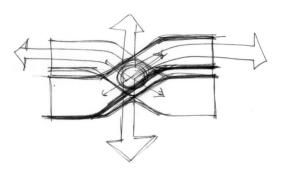

MC *So, the more you talked to the client, the more you realised that both the site and the brief would provide you with a solution for the project itself. I guess this has always been part of your approach: considering the client's desires as a point of departure in the design process.*

KHN Once in Liverpool with the client, we realised they really wanted a building that would be new and bold. They wanted it to be a social place where people, from both Liverpool and further afield, could meet and learn about the city's history. This demanded that the space be flexible and dynamic, facilitating changing exhibitions in the Museum's galleries. The Museum's collection has over 150,000 exhibits, so it was a technical requirement that they be able to be displayed in rotation.

Another thing the client wanted was to have a museum where you could start from the centre of the building and choose your own route to whichever exhibition you wanted to visit. This would obviously provide a certain level of openness given the project as a whole, creating a nodal point from where you could find your own way through the building. This is crucial in the way we work with museums in general, since they have to be used as an educational facility, like Tate Modern or The British Museum, where teachers are able to introduce their students to historical and contemporary culture. So, here we had to create a facility that could also accommodate this kind of visitor flowing through the building. Look closely, and the project is all one big flow — not just a structure — meaning that you can move through the building with ease.

MC *When you started analysing the site in more depth, how did that play into the design of the project? In some of our earlier conversations, you mentioned that, initially, the proposal was going to take the form of a 'bridge'.*

KHN Well, you have to listen to the site and assimilate what it is trying to tell you. At Liverpool, there are very particular characteristics; for instance, the tidal difference is from eight to nine metres, and therefore the controlled docks have become important for leisure activities. At the outset, we did want to make a bridge spanning an underlying dock, but the site sat over a 120 year old railway tunnel, and after a ventilation tunnel was discovered, we chose a plate solution for the building's structure.

We made more than 30 models to study various possible structures, deciding that modelling would help us to better understand the detailed functions and interrelations of the site and its flows. In investigating the Liverpool site, we talked to the public, and travelled around the city by tram and on foot — basically, we tried to experience how people approach the site and how they react to it... what did the site feel like?

MC *This becomes very clear in looking at the flow diagrams — one can see the correlations between those and the Museum on the site.*

KHN It is a direct result of this process, and in that sense, it becomes very functional. Not only does it play with the flow lines and respect the views throughout the area, but it immediately addresses the user. The building starts to function as a natural link, like a geometrical connection between the two main routes through the city.

Intersecting the dramatic tension between urban introspection and the River Mersey's links with the world's oceans, the new Museum of Liverpool lends itself as a connector. It slots into the existing promenade flow along the river; gently without interrupting it. The aim is for people to be able to pass freely through the building without having to integrate into it. For some, it will function as a connecting tool only; others will be engaged by the Museum's displays.

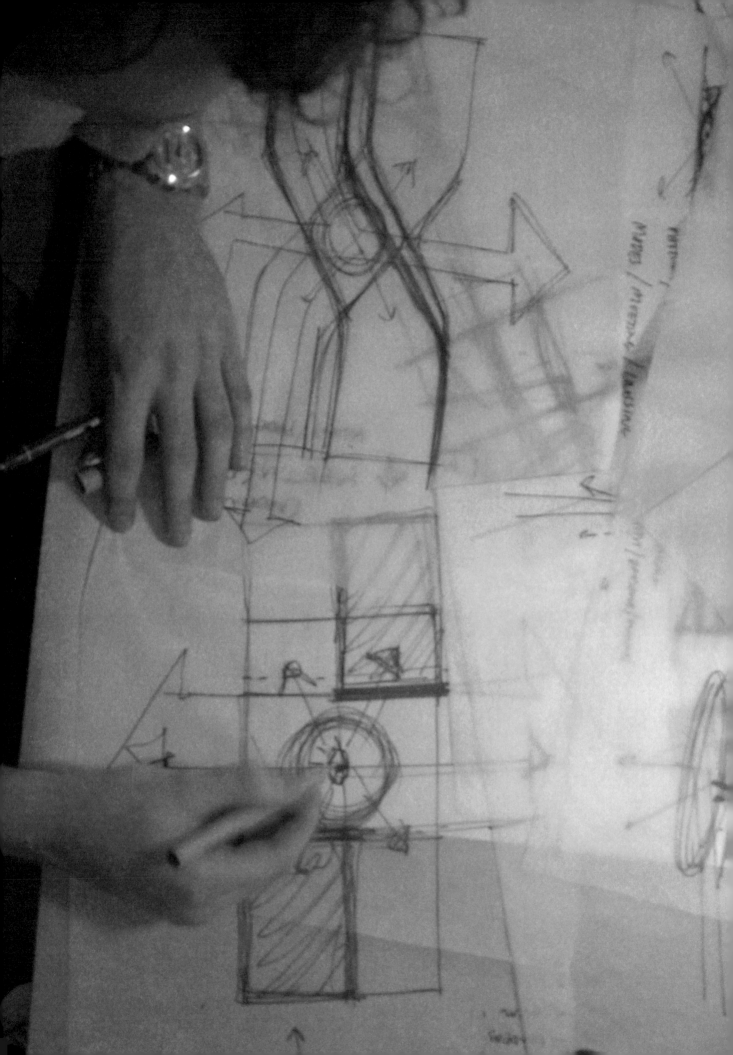

Early models capturing the essential aspects of bridging the flow of the site. The soft lines became straighter during the design phase, because of functional aspects regarding exhibition possibilities, as well as construction requirements.

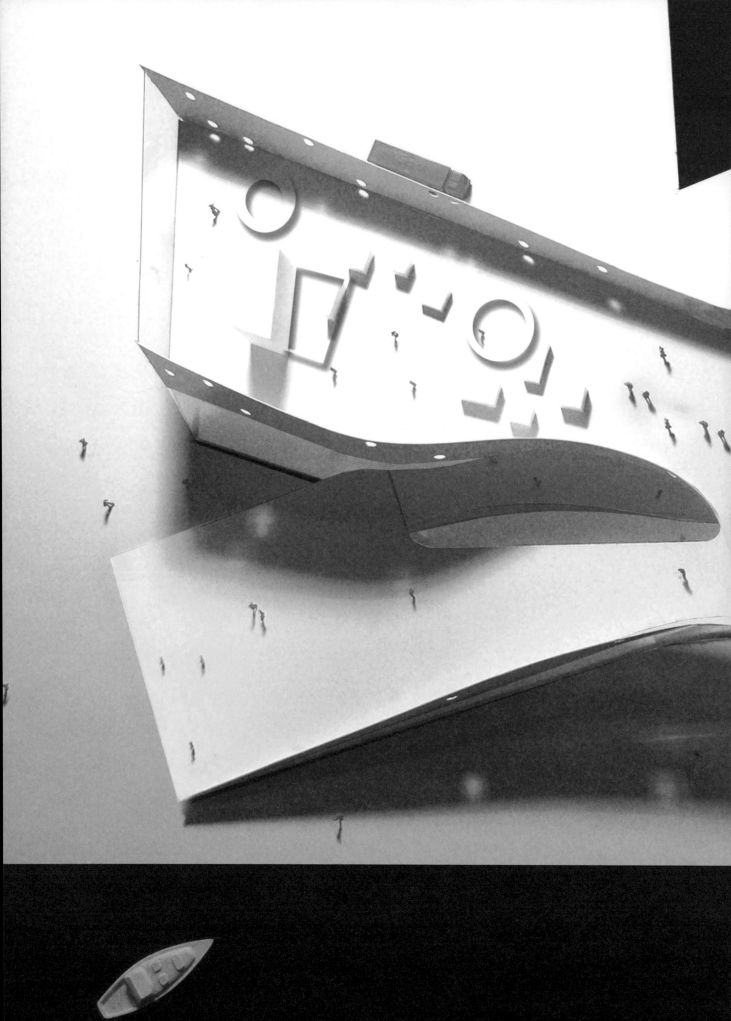

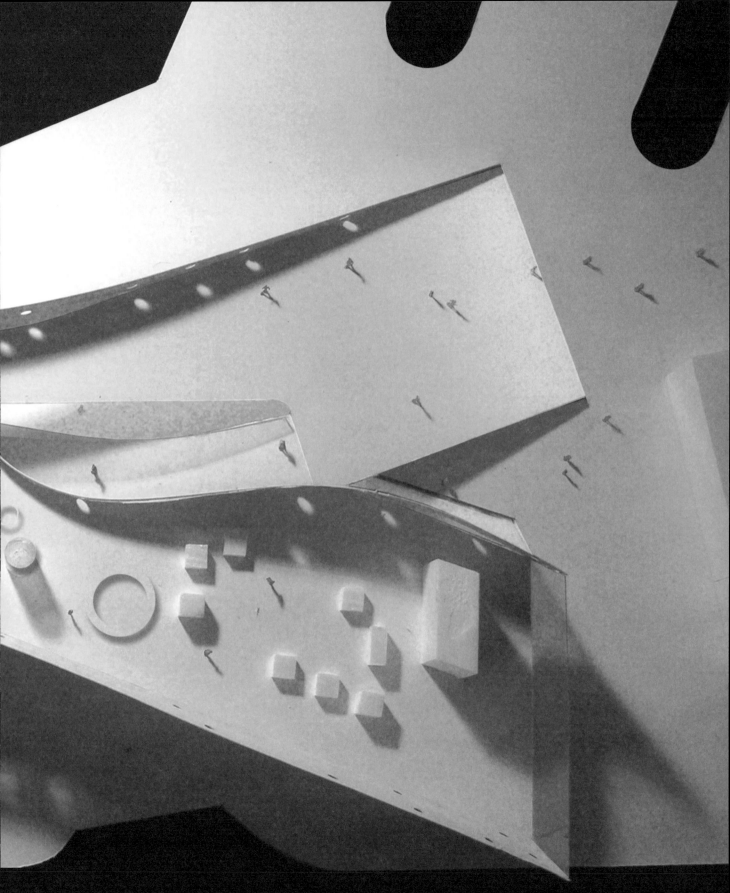

eyeing the city

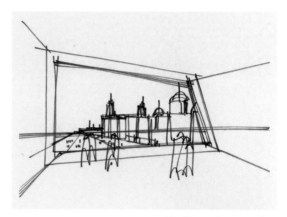

The Museum's panoramic exposure lends itself to 'building in' views of the city and its locations that are echoed by every part of the building — gigantic oculars that point to, focus on and qualify selected historical Liverpool icons. This telescopic function doubles as a 'camera obscura' as these selected views are detached from everyday life and pulled into the interior, which is poignant and illustrative for visitors inside the Museum of Liverpool.

Being a city history museum, it seemed obvious to create visual connections between the city and museum — making the city itself an exhibit.

KHN During discussions with the client, it was made clear that they did not want a closed box. So with this in mind, we designed the Museum so as to enable you to walk through it without having to necessarily enter the building — even the restaurant is placed 'outside' the Museum so as to maintain these routes. The building is also 'see-through', so that from within the Museum you can see outside and vice versa. Framing the view became essential from within the Museum, as did how this 'framing' was perceived externally. Being a city history museum, it seemed obvious to create visual connections between city and museum — making the city itself an exhibit.

Once again, it was a question of dealing with the site and the story it was telling us — and the story that the building should tell. And that's why we controlled the views, so that they could each tell a specific story, but at the same time remain a focal point in themselves.

MC *So, you play with the historical and contextual elements along with the flows and the functions, but*

I also feel it to be a question of being sensitive to the details, and drawing with those in mind. It's all part of the process, responding to the story and the building. "draw" implements the concept even better, especially when you consider the facades. The approach to facades is quite prominent in your work — I can read these as a strong underlying discourse throughout 3XN's entire body of work.

KHN One of the things that hit us was the fact that the Three Graces have very detailed facades. So, we thought we had to carefully elaborate our facades as well. The issue here, however, was in our taking a more abstract approach, working with reliefs on the facades of the Museum. We felt that even the glass should be self-supporting, so that the views would not be obstructed. The more we went into detail, the more sculptural the building became, which meant in turn that the choice of materials became exceedingly important. Every project we undertake is about a dialogue with the site, the function, the people and the surrounding buildings.

In its unique location the new Museum of Liverpool mediates between the city and river, between the static and the dynamic. Liverpudlians use the corridor between the city and river offered by the dock area — the site is overlaid with virtual traces of invisible, well-trodden paths. The unrecorded urban landscape bears clear traces of movement across the site, along the river, skirting the maze of the city.

The building does not just respond to its location, its presence creates, qualifies and delineates spaces for people to pass through or linger in; spaces offering different aspects, views and heights and therefore different moods and possibilities. For example, the expanse of gently rising steps can serve as spectator stands on regatta days in one direction or street performances on the wide pedestrian area in the other.

A

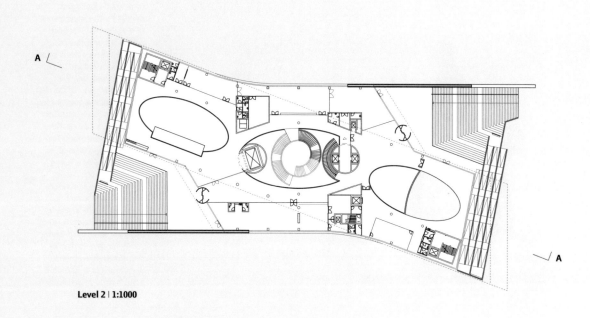

Level 2 | 1:1000

A

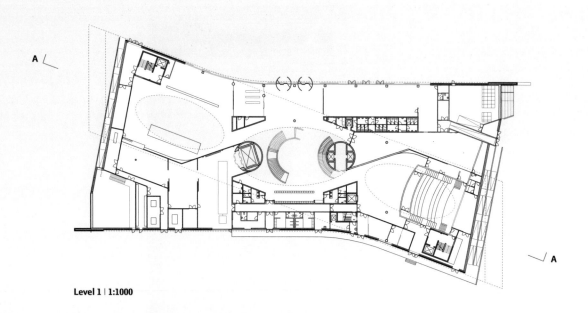

Level 1 | 1:1000

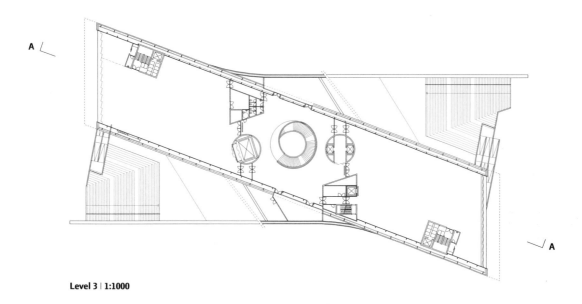

Level 3 | 1:1000

A

A

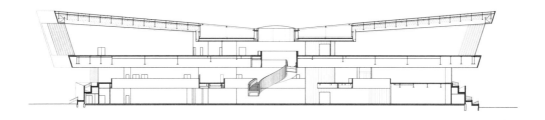

Section AA | 1:1000

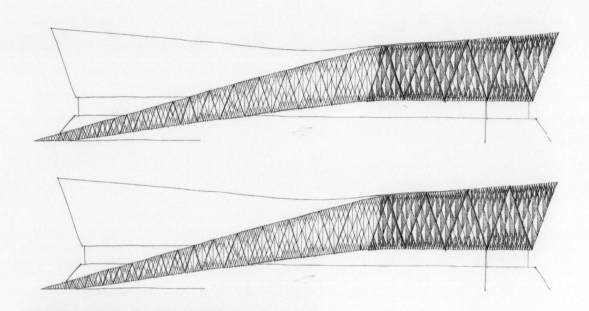

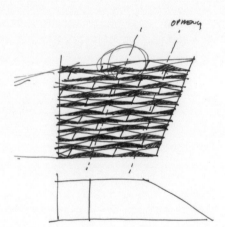

Facade sketches and mock-ups in 1:20 and 1:1. The material palettes of the building and public spaces subtly blend contemporary innovation with references to the existing buildings on the site. At an intimate scale, where visitors are in direct contact with the building, being able to touch and feel the material, the plinth or base of the building is covered in light coloured stone; either jura gelb or travertine.

The 'wings', which shape the main building volume and on a larger scale establish the landmark volume, are clad in a whitish natural stone.

The layout of the stone cladding is set in a geometry where relief, reflections and texture will give the facade a high level of detail, and led to hundreds of sketches like the ones presented here. The mainly transparent glazed first floor is the 'gap' which separates the base and the 'wings'. Several models have been built in scales like 1:100, 1:20, and even 1:1 cardboard models were built to test the relief patterns.

The finally chosen pattern is one that in a subtle way refers to the overall 'nexus' scheme of the building layout.

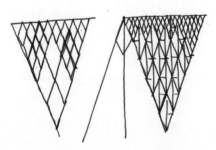

The natural stone facades correspond to those of the Three Graces. Here, Thomas Kâszner inspects a travertine sample that was tested along with a jura gelb stone sample for climate conditions. Jura gelb was the final choice.

Engineer's sketch of foundation considerations. Besides the Manchester Dock and the Chester Basin, the Museum also straddles the Mersey tunnel (historic usage, top; today's situation, bottom).

Though the initial approach was spanning these with a bridge structure, the considerations resulted in flat bed raft foundations that only sit lightly on the ground (construction phase, opposite top; foundation scheme, opposite bottom).

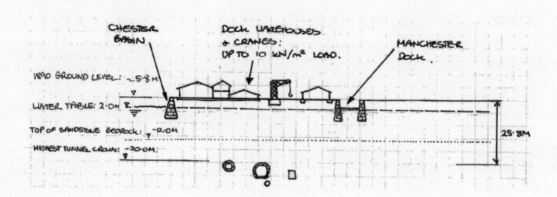

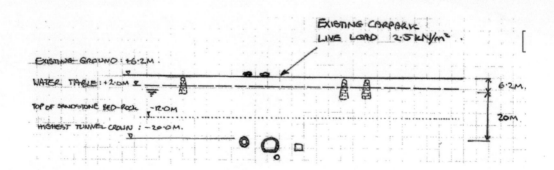

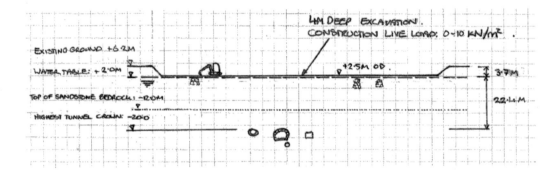

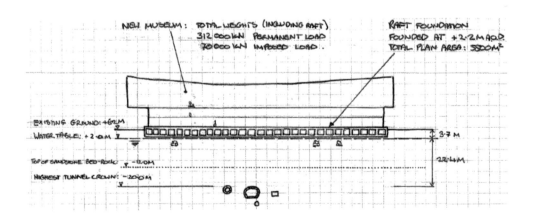

repetition as original

**The organising principle
of the galleries around
the central public forum
allows greatest flexibility
to mix and expand the
range of exhibitions and
activities on offer in the
Museum, and greatest
range of potential for
people engaging with
the Museum. Equally,
the programmatic mix
of the building could be
diversified and expanded,
intensifying use over the
entire day and night, to
appeal to a wider range of
the community.**

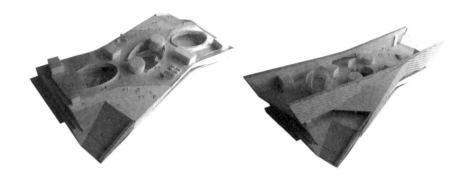

MC *The stairs in the centre of the building are a very
prominent element, and at a first glance I am reminded
of Frank Lloyd Wright's Guggenheim Museum in New
York — and your stair in the Ørestad College. Do you
have, in this regard, an architectural mentor, or an
inspirational figure that has influenced your parcour,
your architectural approach, or is it always the case that
you respond solely to the site and the brief?*

KHN Well, in the early days, we were definitely more
inspired by what was happening around us, but I think
that what we do now is look for a successful solution,
as in the Ørestad College, and when we are faced with
similar problems, we examine solutions that have
worked for us previously as a base for working out the
specific solution for the project in question.

We never thought of the Guggenheim. It's more
that we now build upon our own experience. What
mattered, and what I like most about the Museum, is
that you can easily find your way around it. In many
buildings today, it's actually very hard to do that. We
wanted the project to be logical and for people to find
their way around it without any difficulty.

MC *Do you think that there might be the danger of
certain parts of your work becoming repetitive?*

KHN That might be a problem, but it would be stupid
not to adopt an efficient working solution just for
the sake of doing something different. I think ours is
clearly an architectural language that is determined by
particular requirements. If it was the best solution at
the time, that doesn't mean we will not use it again. But
I agree, too, these should be points of departure from
which you can develop, moving further into a project
and exploring new solutions.

The nexus of the building; the central staircase, is crucial to the Museum, and it was studied thoroughly in sketches, 3-D renders and in physical models. These pages show a small selection of the studies.

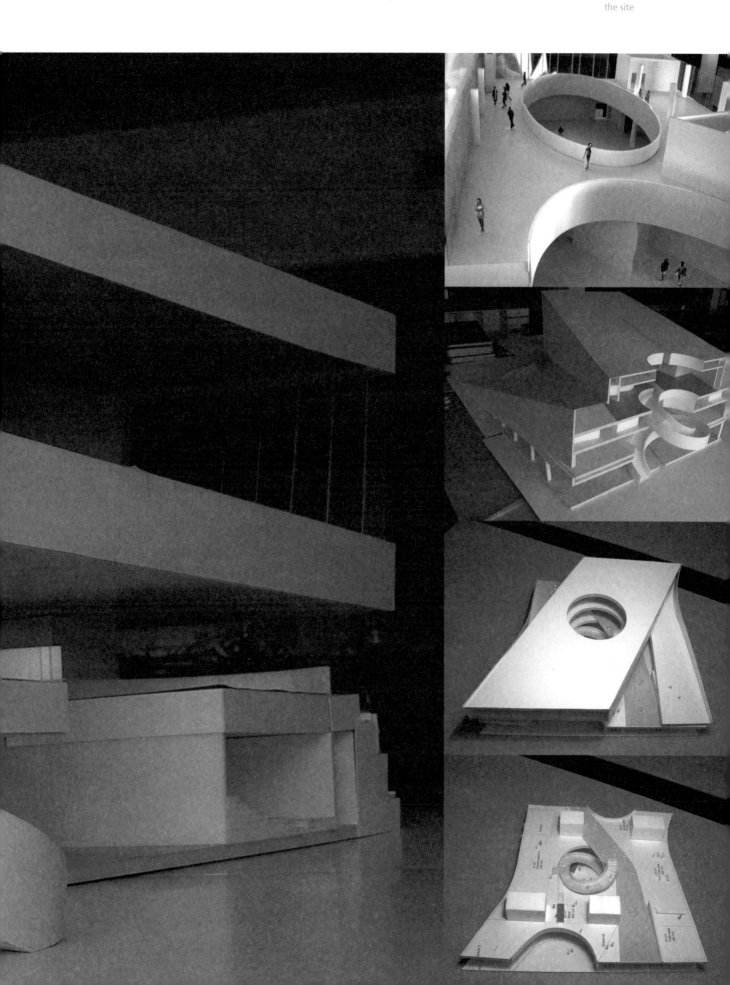

This page and opposite: The atrium serves as public 'living room' as well as entrance lobby, providing connection to the exhibition spaces which are dispersed around it. In this way, the Museum opens towards the outside; a basic condition for interacting with the community.

Look closely, and the project is all one big flow, not just a structure; meaning that you can move through the building with ease.

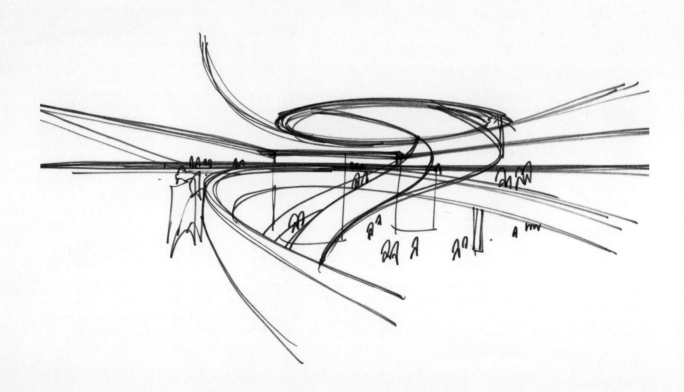

Construction site,
September 2007,
showing the excavation
with foundations and
basement walls.

perpetual
surface

The carpet idea is an appreciative comment on the close relationship in the Danish city of Herning between the textile industry and a unique art collection; the private collection of a shirt manufacturer.

The carpet's precise softness of the two curves emphasises and applauds the professional's expert handling and tactile feel for the material — Herning's own foundations are rooted in the town's great textiles industry.

MC *After all, what is 'original'? Is it really the most important thing? And, in this context, new kinds of solutions have come about using similar processes — as we have previously discussed, investigating the site is part of the process, not just the solution, and the outcome may seem to have little to do with the site.*

For instance, some of your schemes resemble the Moebius strip and its continuous flow strikes me; with their vision of a freeform, continuous space where the floors become walls and the walls become ceiling — all of this is present in both the Rainbow Project and the Liverpool Museum. But even though this is a strong discourse prevalent in architecture today, that is hardly the reason why we find this in 3XN's work?

KHN Well, it has a lot to do with analysing and responding to the flows, especially with the Liverpool Museum, but also in the Rainbow Project, the basis of our proposal was a continuous 'wave', both rhythmical and energetic.

It was an unbroken building with a human dimension — sophisticated and radical, yet soft and friendly. And in the Herning House of Art the idea of a continuous space is taken even more literally — deliberately so, because of certain strong associations with the idea of a carpet, which brings us back to the investigation of the site. Herning is a Danish city, with a long and strong history of producing textiles, and the Museum's collection is in fact based upon a private collection by a successful local shirt producer with a heart for art. A previous building is shaped as a snail, which can be seen as a roll of a carpet viewed from one end, and we wanted to take up and continue this very visual and in some ways naïve or even banal narration. In the end, it also turned out to be a very efficient and logical means to establish the different spatial requirements for an art museum and a concert hall in one building; they are each embraced by a fold of the 'carpet'.

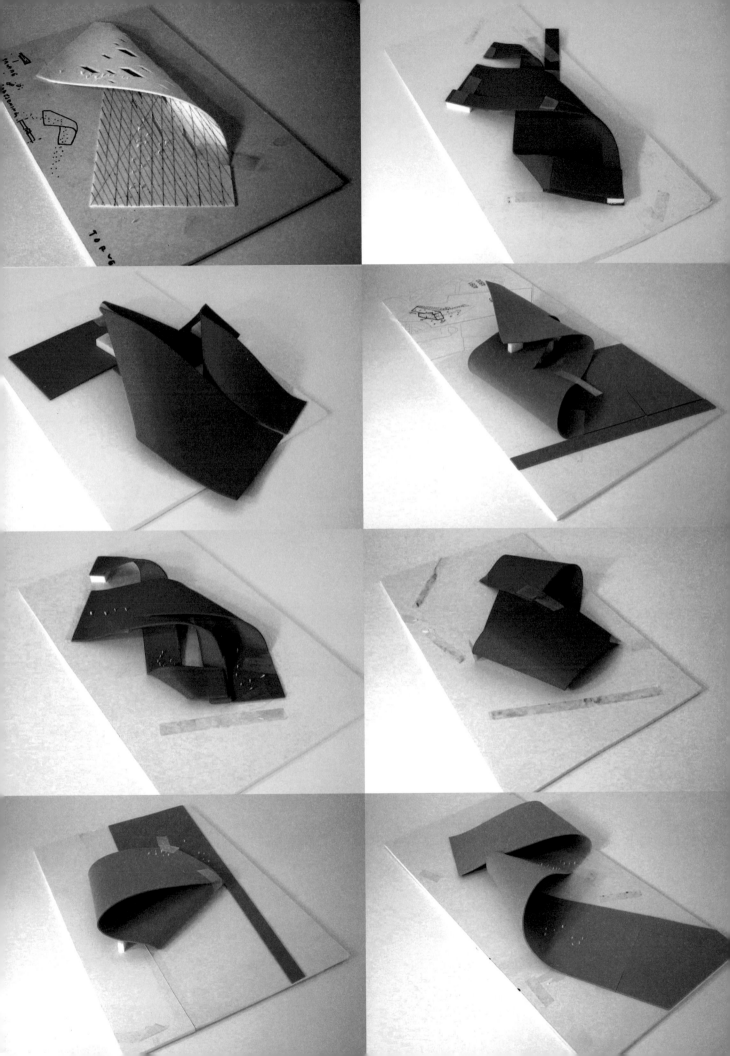

The Herning House of Art does not stand on the ground. The first step of the building *is* the ground: the carpet extends an inviting surface, which then twists upwards in the bold loop of the carpet fold, at first reaching for the skies, then reclining earthwards before looping once again, this time in reverse, and again gliding to earth. The top surface becomes the reverse — and reverts to top surface again. Not in the way of a Moebius strip, closed to the outside world in its own perpetual universe, but as an open, inviting structure linked to the world outside. This flexing movement implies no confrontation with its surroundings, only a co-operative and happy game. With characters formed in space above the ground the movement complements the characters printed on the ground through the supine geometrical elements of the scheme.

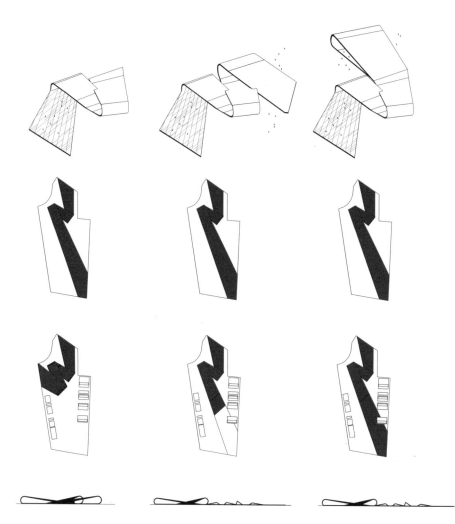

✳ Herning House of Art

A strip of carpet with a couple of soft folds is the simple — yet radical — solution to the Herning House of Art. It embraces the MidWest Ensemble concert hall and Herning Art Museum, along with cafe and restaurant facilities. The carpet concept creates a three-dimensional movement that unites landscape, building and the people who populate these. Despite its strong, definite form, the building is extremely simple — both in its external and internal perception and in its constructive design. Basically, the two folds embrace two halls, which intersect to create a natural common zone. Where the carpet transforms from one fold to the next, it forms the ceiling of a hall as a plane, non-horizontal surface.

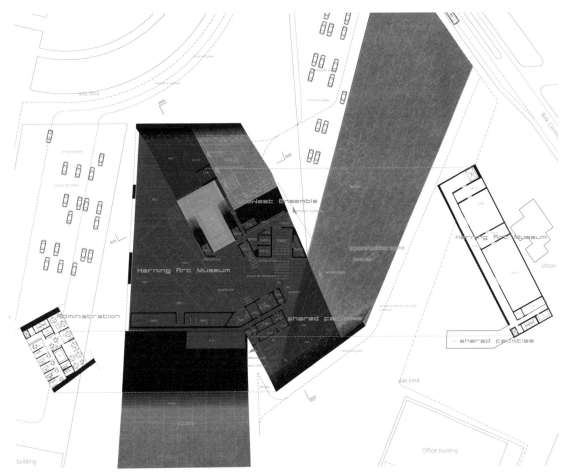

Site plan | no scale

The Lighthouse project. From left: Kim Herforth Nielsen, Ben van Berkel, Michael Kruse and Christian Veddeler at a workshop session in UN Studio's office.

synergy

**UN Studio, 3XN and Gehl,
working on the Lighthouse.**

MC *And you played with this idea in the Renault Project,
too. Here, it's more a topographical surface, but it is still
recognisable. Looking closely at the Liverpool Museum,
Ben Van Berkel also comes to mind. In 1993, he came
up with the Moebius House, which was based on a
double-locked torus; the Moebius strip. In this, I think
you have both interpreted the idea of the Moebius strip
in similar but different ways. And aren't you currently
collaborating with Ben on another project?*

KHN That's right. We actually met when he was part
of the jury for a competition that we eventually
won, and from then on we started discussing how to
collaborate on a project together. He is also part of a
small discussion group I belong to. Once or twice a
year I meet with Ben, Kjetil Thorsen from Snohetta
and Olafur Eliasson to discuss architecture and art. It's
very stimulating. I've already collaborated with Olafur
in the past and now I am working with him on the
Middelfart Savings Bank project. It's quite interesting to
be confronted with another point of view.

MC *The collaboration with Ben has been a successful one,
right? The Lighthouse project is going ahead. And even
here there is a strong emphasis on the site, in this case
Århus' harbourfront.*

KHN The collaboration with Ben has been great, and
it has been mutually respectful. We have avoided the
risk in all collaborations; that you end up with a poor
compromise. We remember who is who, and in this case
it has been pure synergy! The project is, again, about
the investigation of the site. It is not an architecture of
landscape, like the Dublin Rainbow or the Liverpool
project, but more about working within the typology of
a traditional block structure, and how to transform this.
Here, we concentrated more on how to divide the space,
and less on how it be shaped. Our concern was that it be
functional and in keeping with the spirit of the site. The
orientation was very important because of the views,
the winds and all of the other site characteristics. The
'site' is actually water right now, and the reflection of
lights in water is also part of the interpretation. One of
our major discussions, though, was about how to ensure
that everybody had a view out towards the sea — to the
north — as well as views to the city core, and to provide
functional outdoor spaces.

✳ The Lighthouse

The Lighthouse project will feature Denmark's tallest building and contain the unconventional mixture of luxury private apartments and non-profit housing. This way, the project facilitates social diversity and access to the attractive residences for middle-income groups and ensures a healthy balance in the new district.

The architecture theme has been to establish an overall homogeneity combined with many variations. It is created especially for this place and for this city, and has been developed in close cooperation between 3XN, the Dutch architects UN Studio and the urban environment experts Gehl Architects. It was developed with thorough studies of the societal development, cultural trends and living conditions, the marvellous location of the area, as well as considerations of wind and weather conditions.

The development project consists of housing facilities of approximately 40,000 square metres and commercial facilities of approximately 20,000 square metres. There will be 400 residences, of which 100 will be non-profit rental residences and 300 will be owner-occupied residences (of these approximately 270 flats and 30 terraced houses).

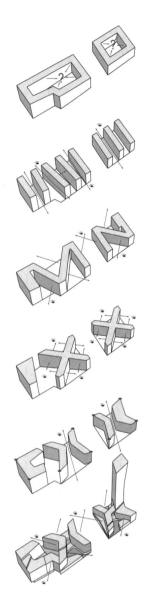

A developing sequence explaining how the design was taken from the masterplan's traditional block structure to disconnected X-shapes. The manoeuvres aimed at providing everyone with a view to the sea, as well as to the harbour environment to the opposite side (red arrows illustrate possible view lines), without losing a grip of the corners that the original blocks touched (red dots on illustration second from bottom).

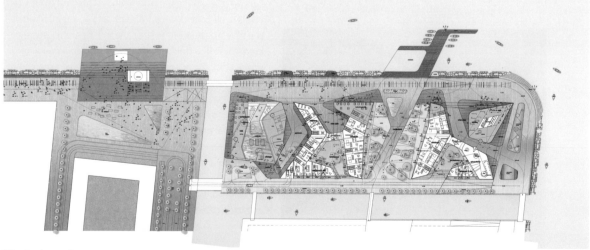

Site plan | no scale

View from the canal to the city side (top), from the city along the seaside promenade (bottom left) and from the top sky bar in the tower towards the city of Århus (bottom right).

Programme

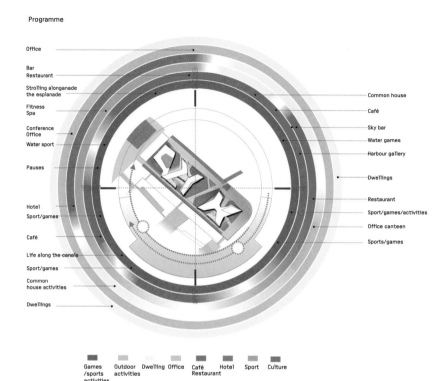

Office
Bar
Restaurant
Strolling alonganade
the esplanade
Fitness
Spa
Conference
Office
Water sport
Pauses
Hotel
Sport/games
Café
Life along the canals
Sport/games
Common
house activities
Dwellings

Common house
Café
Sky bar
Water games
Harbour gallery
Dwellings
Restaurant
Sport/games/activities
Office canteen
Sports/games

Games
/sports
activities
Outdoor
activities
Dwelling
Office
Café
Restaurant
Hotel
Sport
Culture

Diversity in all its forms and life 24/7 played a major part in the process, inseparable from the site's obvious qualities. Many new harbour developments suffer from lifelessness and desolation. This project assembles people in compact, precisely defined and carefully designed urban spaces that combine necessary, everyday urban life with the free-choice of urban leisure life.

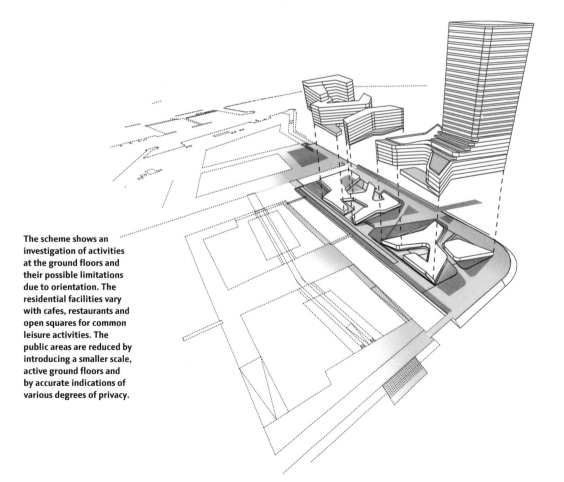

The scheme shows an investigation of activities at the ground floors and their possible limitations due to orientation. The residential facilities vary with cafes, restaurants and open squares for common leisure activities. The public areas are reduced by introducing a smaller scale, active ground floors and by accurate indications of various degrees of privacy.

The characteristic patterns
of the facades mirror the
reflections of light in
water, and have undergone
many studies, including
biological structures and
patterns. See overleaf.

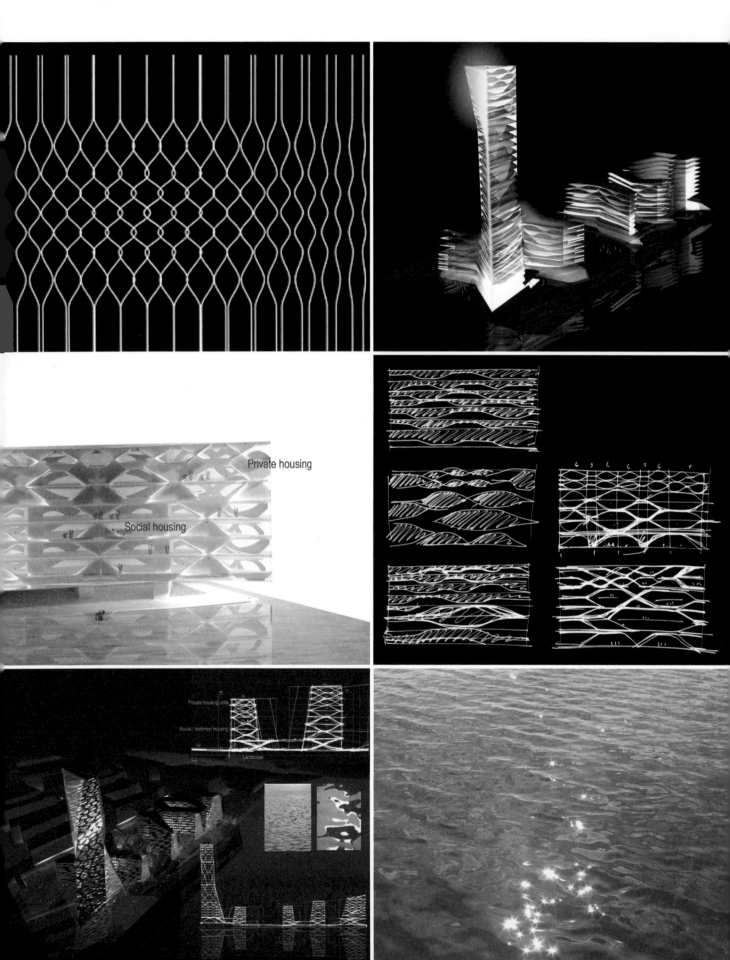

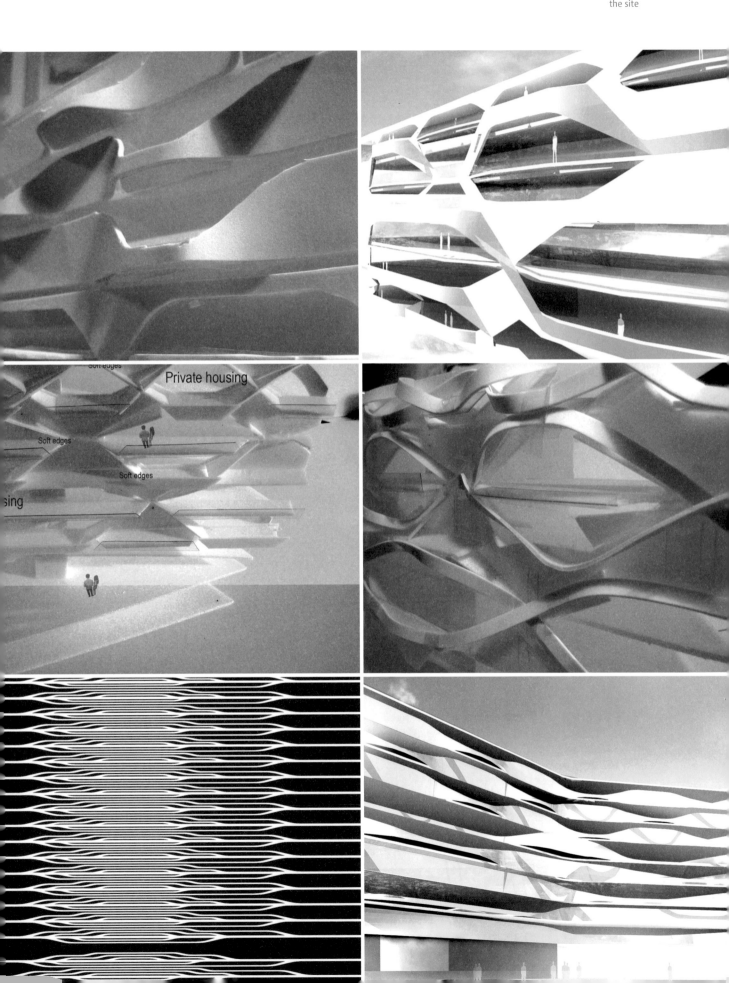

wind

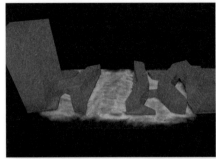

The basic idea here was to provide all residents with access to the sun from the south and the view to the north, to the sea. It is about 'living the view'. This means that the buildings will only have fronts, with no rear views.

This desired openness, however, might have collided with the sometimes strong sea winds. Wind tunnel experiments were carried out to find the best way to create protected places close to the buildings, in order to achieve a soft zone between public and private. This was part of the background for the two-storey terrace houses that extend from the main buildings (bottom).

MC *And as the site is right on the sea-side, the influence of the wind must have been taken into account.*

KHN The wind did play a big part in our developing the scheme. We worked with wind tunnel testing, and benefited from the insights these studies brought to the scheme. But the question of lighting and orientation was also important, so investigations of the site characteristics were essential in the development of the project. The important thing was that we wanted the project to work as a whole. We then went on to study how people would sit in the open areas, so that these would be areas of interaction. Also important here was where to place the commercial spaces, how to enter the site, and how to provide car access to it. The purpose here was to build a community, meaning that we

wanted to bring people together, and for this to happen successfully, we had to take into account every possible aspect of the scheme.

MC *In that sense, you are creating a landmark building that will be more than just an icon.*

KHN It is. Initially the tower was going to be 110 metres, then 150, and now it is 142. It is definitely going to be a landmark for Århus and it's going to be telling the story of the city. We wanted a building that would react to and take references from the city, and not just copy Dutch harbour developments, as they are doing in Copenhagen. This is going to be a landmark for Århus and it's going to be telling a story. In this context, the whole facade plays a significant part, with a clear reference being made to light's reflection in the waves.

The overall impression will be green in the lower levels of the complex. The facades have two layers, woven together to one entity, in a material that serves several purposes: as climate screen, load-carrier, visual protection — and as a general provider of a connecting identity with many possibilities for variations.

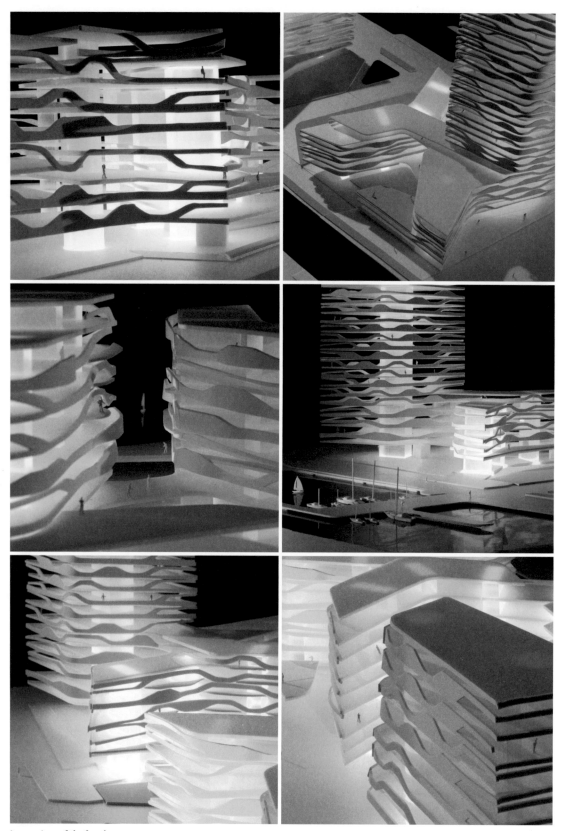

**Impressions of the facade
structure, tested as a
physical model in different
lighting conditions.**

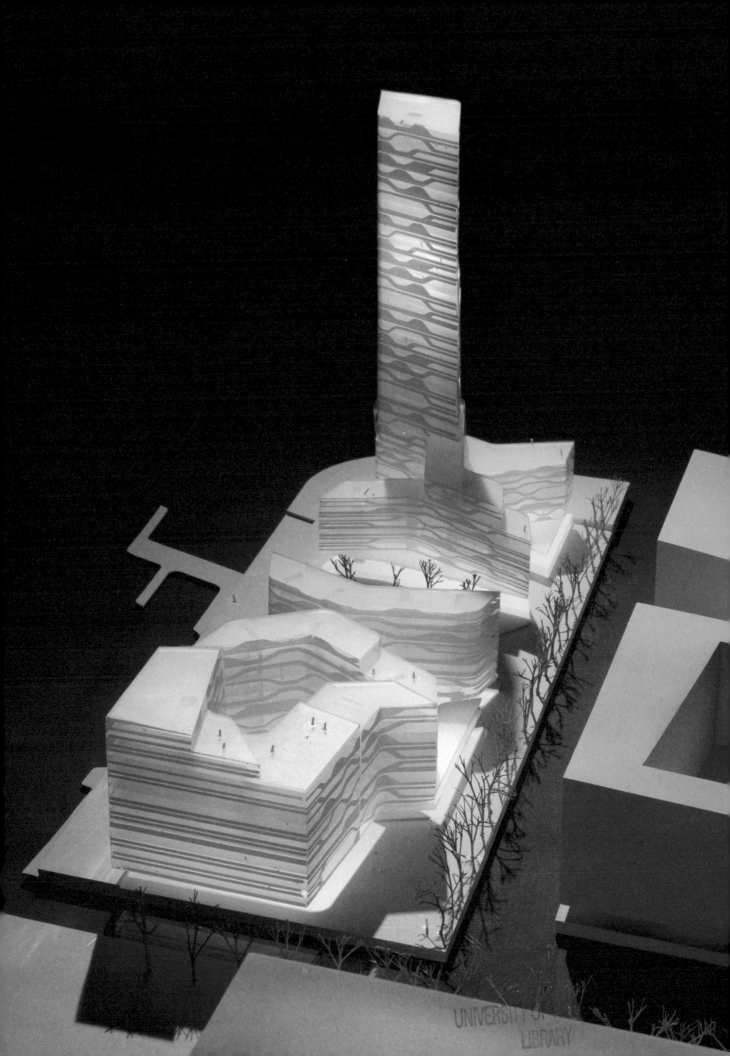

part of the landscape

Kristiansand Music and Theatre Centre prolongs the contour of the mountain, which so remarkably characterises Odderøya (Otter Island). The building extends its bow towards the water, connected at places to the rock. It provides the transition between the flat silo quay and the dramatic landscape, not only visually, but also physically with the set of ramps that brings people up and down in soft movements.

The situation is being developed on its own terms, resulting in a unique design. The new urban platform is a natural point of view, offering a full coastal panorama to the sea and to Kristiansand.

MC *Reaction to the site has really been the opening discourse in this process, and your ability to interact and respond to it has brought diverse results. In some cases, it is a question of integration, and in others creating an aggregating element, or better still, a regenerative one.*
KHN Well, it also depends on the brief. If you think about the Kristiansand Theatre, it is a fairly big building in a very small town. They wanted a building to use for concerts and theatre. The solutions could have been multiple, but the important aspect here was how to bring about this scheme in the area and get the scale right. The site was significant and, in that sense, the solution we adopted was to make the building a part of the landscape. However, the real issue was that the building had to be used in more than one way; it had to be a contemporary solution where connections and uses could be adapted to changing demand.
MC *So, in the end, it is all about such demands, and how one approaches these, and here 3XN's approach is what makes a difference. It isn't just about investigating the site but also asking the people, telling the story and building a project that is able to respond to diverse needs.*

KHN The site and the research are part of the process, but as you mentioned, clients have a major role to play in all of this. Even to projects like the Ørestad College, where dialogue with the client was important, the site was essential. We had to condense the building on the site. The original brief for the block where the College is situated left no place for any open green spaces. The masterplan for this block was part of the competition, and we immediately decided to try and incorporate such a common space in the heart of the site for social interaction outdoors.

Everything comes into play, and one has to find a point of departure. But this doesn't mean that there can't be overlaps or diversions, especially if this means coming up with better solutions.

✳ Kristiansand Theatre

The Music and Theatre Centre in Kristiansand is an urban cultural institution, but the special topography around this southern Norwegian city made it natural to choose a far from urban setting — the Odderøya (Otter Island); one of the small islands in the waters at Kristiansand, which is connected to the mainland by a dam.

The point of inspiration in this competition proposal is the rocks of Odderøya. The building prolongs the contour of the mountain, which so remarkably characterises this island, and it merges imperceptibly with the winding coastline and encourages a dynamic contrast to the habitual grid-structure of Kristiansand. The structure provides the transition from the flat silo quay to the dramatic landscape's

mountain tops, not only visually, but also physically, with the set of ramps that bring people up and down in soft movements. The site's unique characteristics are used on their own terms, resulting in a unique design. The new urban platform is a natural point of view, offering a full coastal panorama to the sea and to Kristiansand.

At night, the audience will appear as silhouettes at foyer decks in various heights, participating and performing in an unwritten choreography, each night anew. A curved front opens the public foyers towards the water and the view, while the technical areas to the concave back are concentrated, resulting in short transportation lines and clear logistics. The curved shape creates smaller v-shaped open 'stages' between the three

concert halls; undefined and therefore open to interpretations.

Three different halls define the ensemble. In the concert hall, the theatre hall and the multi-functional hall the experience — not least the acoustics — is the focal point. The theatre hall layout aims at intense intimacy between players and spectators. The multi-functional hall is situated centrally between theatre and concert hall. This hall can be opened widely towards the surrounding foyer decks, and this feature makes it possible to place the performers on the foyer decks and the audience inside the hall, sitting on the stage. This way the building becomes a tool for the stage designer's imagination, and opens for a complete integration between architecture and art.

The foyer can be used traditionally as meeting point and circulation area.

The foyer can become a place for the audience when the space is opened in this way.

**The Kristiansand Theatre
and Music Centre has that
presence and can respond
to the challenges of the
large ships docked nearby.**

ask

the people

dialogue

MC *The master planning of the site played a huge role in the Ørestad College competition, but you were telling me that it was all related to the dialogue between yourselves, the users and the client. The idea of sublimating your own desires to understand that of someone else's is very attractive. This must also relate to maturity professionally as well as personally. Can you explain the development within 3XN — and in yourself?*

KHN It was always about dialogue, one way or another. When the three of us originally started the practice in 1986, it was because we had a lot in common and we wanted to work together. We would meet and discuss architecture; we criticised our own work, which was stimulating. But, like a marriage, things were difficult and with time we kind of grew apart, each deciding to go his own way. Hans Peter left first to follow a more theoretical path, while Lars Frank stayed until just three years ago. The open and constructive dialogue was the most vivid part of our architecture up until that point, and luckily we also managed to separate in a positive atmosphere.

MC *How do you feel about being the sole remaining principal of the former trio? Do you have the feeling of a fresh start?*

KHN That's it! At the end, instead of helping each other, our relationship became a constraint. When I was left with the full responsibility, we started anew with the Ørestad College as the stepping-stone. That project for me is a symbol of a fresh start, where I found a new energy within the practice.

MC *So now, how does your office work? Is it more about you and your approach or do you have a dialogue with the people around you? Is there a specific hierarchy within your office, or does everyone work at a similar level?*

KHN It is a combined approach. I definitely give direction to the architecture, but this comes about through dialogue. It's more about our approach to work. It's about having a dialogue that then contributes to solving problems.

MC *Would you agree that much current thinking is not about solving problems but creating them? Or is it as Marcel Duchamp said, "there is no solution because there is no problem"?*

KHN I would simply say that 3XN's architecture is based, in part, on dialogue. I engage in dialogue, and what results is a dialogue. It is this spirit of creating architecture in which I discuss issues with the people I am close to — no one specific in the office; it's more like a series of conversations that generate ideas, and these conversations may involve new as well as old, trusted employees. The content of these talks are important to me — not who said what and how. For me, style is not an issue — like Jean-Luc Godard once said, "style is the outside of the content"!

Kim Herforth Nielsen and
Tommy Bruun discussing
planning strategies for a
project in France.

Working models, Ørestad College (this page and opposite, bottom).

programming

The spiral motif is emblematic of the aims and concept for the Ørestad College; uniting mathematics, natural science, history and aesthetics.

MC *So, in your case, you are the driving force, setting the direction for the practice. But, at the same time, it is important to interact. To quote another film director, Milos Forman once said that his cameraman was a better cameraman than he was; and actors can act in a way that he cannot; and the soundman records the sound; so what am I, the director? In the end, he is the one who will bring it all together. For you, is that what being an architect is all about, bringing together diverging ideas and disciplines in a unified and logical way?*

KHN A relevant question — what you are really asking about is leadership. The architect is the driving force of the process and must listen and understand even the smallest sound, noise or whisper. He brings professionals together, and contributes as well. You have to become more and more sensitive. Architecture is interpretive. And in this we have chosen not to make signature architecture. Our approach is not premeditative. Of course, we welcome appropriate credit, but mainly for the way we treat problems, rather than a concern for early ideas about appearance. 3XN is not about 'wallpaper' architecture. This is a problem for many architects; they find a signature style and then stick with it, while in reality, architecture is more of a circular and dynamic process, addressing many parties and parameters.

MC *I agree, it's more about ideas and a way of thinking. But sometimes, it is the client that creates a problem, in that if they love a particular project, they want something that is similar for themselves. This is something of the trap of style. A good client is someone*

with a dream, a strong desire, and who is not afraid to take risks with the architecture.

KHN Yes, and who has confidence in the architect! In that sense, I think the client for the Ørestad College was precisely what we needed. The competition was all about new ways to design a school. The brief was the building — no more defined classrooms, nothing but open space.

MC *In the competition for the College, you were up against Dominique Perrault, Massimiliano Fuksas, Sauerbruch Hutton, and three Danish architects — and you won...*

KHN Yes, but before the Copenhagen Municipality started the competition for the College they asked three architectural firms to work on a new way of 'programming' the school. And one of the curious things here is that all of this happened before the actual law reform of the Danish upper secondary education was passed. The political agreement was reached in 2003, and in August 2005 the first students met the practical consequences of this. Amongst these changes were the elimination of the traditional division between science and the humanities, the emphasis being put on interdisciplinary work, flexibility and varying working and studying methods.

Our response to the brief, including the classrooms being considered zones, was the one finally adopted. It was a true depiction of what the client really wanted. And with this programme, they finalised the drafting of the reforms. In fact, instead of 1,000 words, our 'model' became the basis of the new law.

✳ Ørestad College

The Ørestad College is the newest 'gymnasium' (college or upper secondary school) in Copenhagen. It is built in the Danish capital's development area; Ørestad. The demographic development in greater Copenhagen has resulted in a remarkable growth of the 16–19 year group, with Copenhagen needing 50 per cent more study places, and this led to a decision to build a new college in Ørestad City; the new city centre for the entire Ørestad area.

Ørestad College offers fields of study within science, social science and human science. The purpose of the college is to realise the latest reforms' (2005) aims to strengthen and renew the students' professional capabilities, to prepare the students better for university and to enhance the science aspect. This College has chosen a profile of media, communication and culture, with wireless Internet all over the school and with laptops for all students — hence the knick-name the Virtual College.

The brief was deliberately formulated without traditional terms for rooms, and left much to the architects' interpretation. The proposal was therefore not so much a response to a specifically defined task as an element in the necessary development of the idea of a Danish college.

Four boomerang shaped storey decks rotate in relation to each other like the shutter of a camera. They form the superstructure; the overall framework of the College, and provide space for the College's four study zones. Each zone is on one level, providing organisational flexibility, with the option of micro adjustment to create different spaces, learning environments and group sizes. The rotation of the storey decks projects a part of each deck into the high central hall. This part is the so-called X-zone; a spatial expression of the College's ambition to promote interdisciplinary expertise between study zones with physical and visual links.

The storey decks are open towards a central core, where a broad main staircase winds its way upwards to the roof terrace. The main staircase is the heart of college educational and social life; the primary connection up and down, but also a place to stay, watch and be seen. Three 'mega columns' form the primary load bearing system, supplemented by a number of smaller columns positioned according to structural requirement, not as part of a regular grid. As a result, each floor has few permanent elements and can be laid out and rearranged almost completely at will.

The main staircase binds the entire building together, along with the protruding 'shelves'. The 'drums' are elements that serve several purposes — they are supplied with secondary stairs to connect two floors, but they also contain spaces inside them that can be isolated or integrated at will, and on top they have places for contemplation, relaxing or conversations, stretched out in bean bag chairs in selected colours.

The superstructure is supplemented by a series of newly developed 'room furniture', which accommodate the need for the flexible and temporary room arrangements and learning environments required by varying group sizes — from one on one to an entire cohort.

The rotated decks are mirrored in the facades. Due to their rotation, the decks create double- and triple-height openings while drawing lines on the facade. As a rule, the glass is smooth with the deck fronts, but on each floor, one facade is withdrawn to create outdoor space. These outdoor spaces are connected from ground to roof. In front of the glass facades, a series of coloured semi-transparent glass louvers can open or close to protect from the sun, while adding dashes of colour to the indoor environment.

overlapping spaces

Programming: the built area can be reduced by introducing 'lean' thinking and 'just-in-time' flexible spaces. Foam blocks illustrating a full functional programme, if running concurrently, with no regards to timewise distribution.

The College is all about continuous interaction, where the entire space is multi-functional — nothing is fixed, so that students and teachers are given a new flexibility.

ᴍᴄ *You mentioned that the College was a success, and is now the most popular in the area — and this was even before building started.*

ᴋʜɴ Yes. And one of the positive things we did here was to 'condense' the building on the site. And as the master planning was part of the competition, the site investigation provided a starting point.

ᴍᴄ *So, the College is about the relationship between students and teachers — in that learning is about curiosity and ideas, not intimidation.*

ᴋʜɴ Initially, it was also about the relationship between us, the architects and the client. We tried to establish a dialogue from the beginning. The competition brief was deliberately very open, so it was necessary to develop the proposal further in close cooperation with the building's users. At the outset of the process, the client brought in a group of five or six teachers, with us writing down the entire brief — and that started our discussions. Through these conversations, and many other meetings, we slowly started to solve the brief's problems. Without these discussions, the project simply couldn't have progressed — so the dialogue was essential for all of us. In our model here, one can really see all the functions needed on each floor — and as you can see, there is no space for moving around. We needed to introduce overlapping and shared spaces to create room enough for the entire brief. And this was one of the interesting and most important parts to the scheme; that is, how the various groups within the College might interact. In the end, ours was a rather open proposal that was subject to change and discussion, since the brief itself had set down only the

Zone area
Principle

Zone area
Adaptation to form

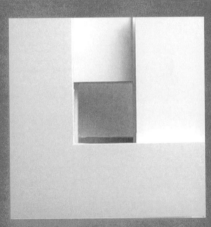

Overlapping zones
Principle — visual/physical connections

Overlapping zones
Dynamic spatial evolution — movement

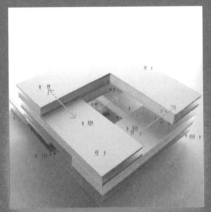

Interdisciplinary relations
Principle — openness and light

Interdisciplinary relations
Adaptation to form — character and identity

fact that there should be three divisions — which might
be departments (science, creative/music or media) or
age groups.

MC *So, is it by asking and confronting people with ideas
and propositions that the everyday user is turned into a
true client?*

KHN That's right. And in that sense, the consultations
with the students and teachers took on an essential
role in the development of the College's design.
Furthermore, our approach here came to inform what
has become a key project, in that it represents a new era
of educational reform in Denmark.

The essential thing to understand here, though, is
that in this building every square inch of space is being
used; the athletic area can be used for theatre, the
last prom, teaching or even as a restaurant/bar. Even
the corridor that connects the technical spaces in the
basement (the only corridor in the building!) can be
used as a running track. It has rounded corners and
doubles as an extension to the sports area. The College
is all about continuous interaction, where the entire
space is multi-functional — nothing is fixed, so that
students and teachers are given a new flexibility.

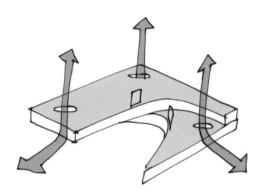

The College has three
levels of vertical
connections: The main
winding staircase in the
centre (below); staircases
that connect the X-zones
via the 'drums' (opposite,
working model); and
finally the escape routes
concealed inside the three
'mega'-columns (above,
competition diagram).

Expected openness and
transparency in the central
atrium; competition render.

Each floor level has a study, introduction and workshop area along with an open area; the X-zone (above). From the centre to the facades, dynamic activity is gradually transformed to contemplative concentration (detailed working model, opposite).

The floor levels overlap, leaving the X-zone visible up through the atrium. Levels may be divided on the basis of age or on a study field basis.

A cubicle outline contrasts the softly moulded interior. This fits the condensed site and sits up against the grand scale of the context.

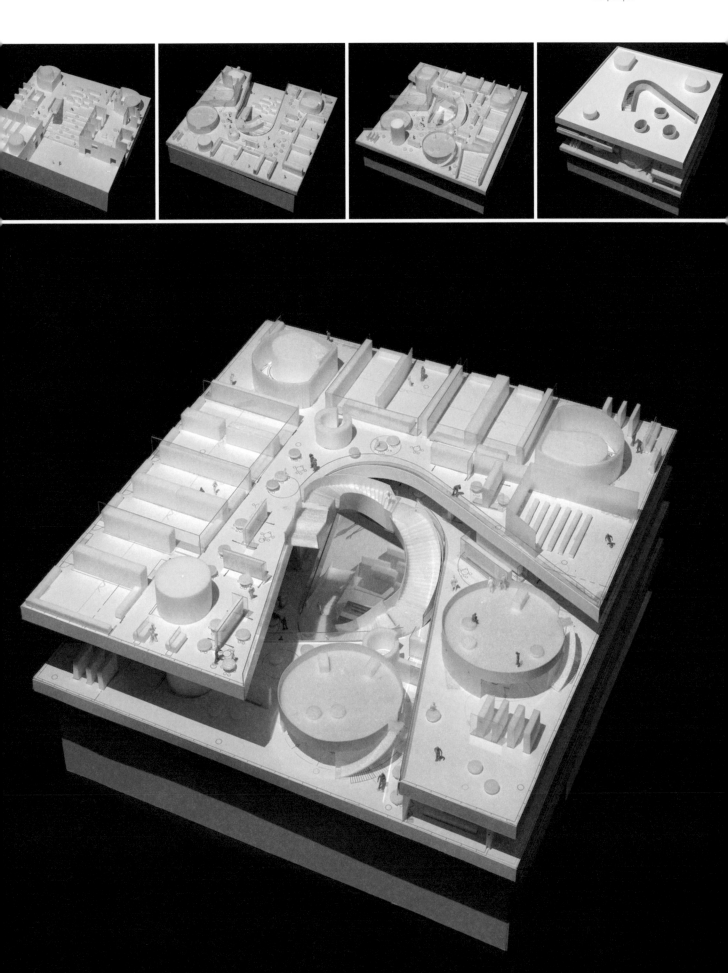

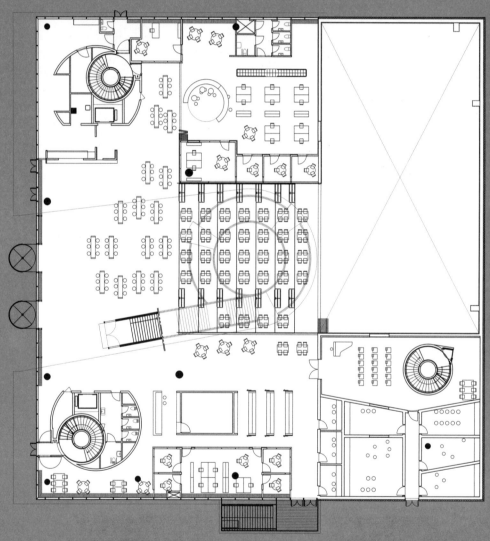

Level 0 | 1:400

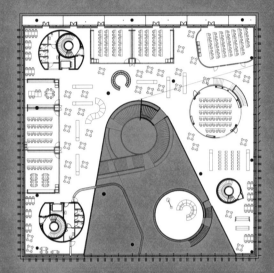

Level 2 | 1:800

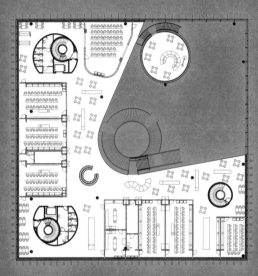

Level 4 | 1:800

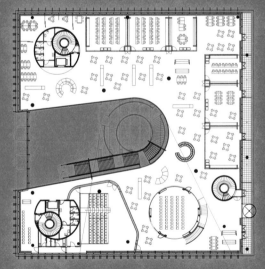

Level 1 | 1:800

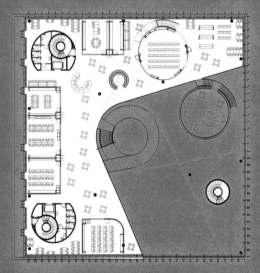

Level 3 | 1:800

The Ørestad College competition also comprised a masterplan for the entire block. This opened the possibility to control the immediate surroundings: a parking garage, a library extension and sports facilities are integrated into an artificial landscape in order to establish an outdoor green area. Working model.

creating behaviour

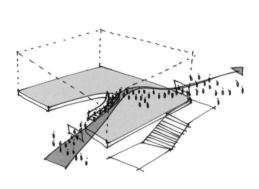

The building is open to a through-flow from the entrance level, moving up one level and exiting to the green area inside the block.

The spiral staircase is planned as the central meeting place. It is designed to be much wider than mere transportation needs require; it becomes a space in itself.

MC *And within the space, the most impressive element is the spiral staircase. It connects the entire space vertically and, in a way, even horizontally. How did you come up with it?*

KHN We made, I believe, about 20 different models, but the main idea is that of overlapping and shared spaces. The staircase is where everybody has to pass, so as to circulate through the building. People meet and are able to interact and exchange information.

This is the idea of a meeting space as the node of an internal network — not a form of connection, but a space in itself.

It is a space of interaction, which is why we made it so wide. It becomes the focal point. The school has 800 students, which means there are a lot of people walking up and down the stair. It has been very exciting to see how they interact; on the central stairs as well in, for instance, the lounge areas on top of the drums. The other advantage of this stair is that one enters each

area more or less in the building's centre. This ensures that the largest possible area on each floor is without through traffic.

MC *Looking at the project, you realise that it has very interesting spaces. For example, the spaces on top of the 'barrels'; lounge areas where students can relax, meet and interact. This building makes me feel as though there is really a warmth to the architecture, almost a kind of cosiness to it. It's not a cold, steel and glass box. The architecture is not trying to be an icon or precious building, but something welcoming to the students and teachers who work there.*

KHN Yes, for me architecture is more about creating spaces and environments that accommodate the people working and living in them. All through the process it has been important to us as well as the client to have an environment that is inspiring and designed with the human being in full focus. I believe that architecture creates behaviour.

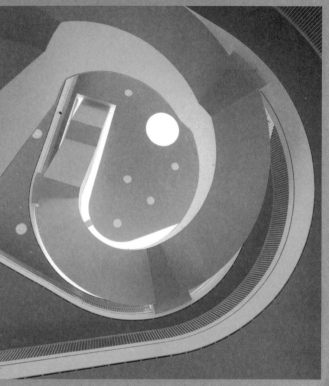

The central staircase
reaches to the roof where a
verdant terrace is planned.

All through the process it has been important to us, as well as the client, to have an environment that is inspiring and designed with the human being in full focus.

From detail to the larger picture: the overall floor plan layout of the College (central staircase, left) is fine-tuned and supplied with specially designed furniture that also has an impact on behaviour and culture (locker drum, below).

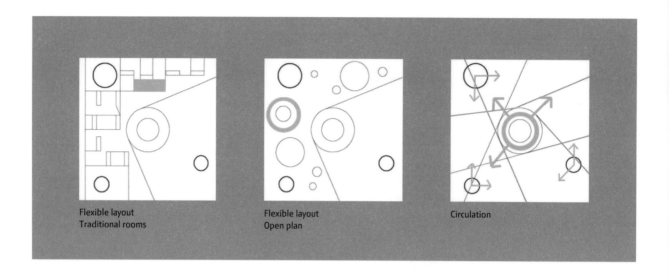

Flexible layout
Traditional rooms

Flexible layout
Open plan

Circulation

800 students are in the Ørestad College on a daily basis, and obviously, noise has been an issue. However, in spite of the open environment, the careful considerations to acoustics have been successful. The acoustic climate is created by computer simulation of the open areas (auralisation) pointing out ceilings and vertical surfaces as acoustic absorbers. The overall acoustic ambience differs from area to area but creates a calm and pleasant atmosphere.

The transparent space makes the many different education situations visible on a mutual basis, both group teaching and teamwork.

transparency

Physics class.

We created an almost columnless space. This allows for a high degree of flexibility and transparency.

MC *I am reminded here of Alain de Botton's book,* The Architecture of Happiness, *wherein he describes how we are influenced by the quality of our surroundings and the fundamental role these play in our well-being. This was already something Marcel Breuer had in mind in his attempt to make people feel at home in his buildings. However, today this often doesn't seems to be the case. On the contrary, architecture aligns itself with extravagance, and there is often no dialogue between the architect and a building's occupants. This is what appears to be so different in the Danish architectural approach, even at the level of the smallest detail.*

KHN That's true, and it is really important to us, right down to every detail in a building. And in this, the acoustics are also very important, as these ultimately enable you to communicate. Even designing the furniture became essential. We did a workshop with an artist, which resulted in the idea of screens being part of the scheme — these allow you to see what is happening around you and to plug yourself in to see where your courses will be on a given day. Students choose their own studies, and there are no specific classes. This is all about the idea of incorporating technology in the building, of being up-to-date with the demands of the new generation.

In other words, it is a free-moving space, where the staircase holds it all together. The transparency of the facade and the freedom from structural constraints within the space all play a part in this.

We created an almost columnless space. This allows for a high degree of flexibility and transparency, but has also called for special solutions. For instance, all the services come up through the 'mega-columns' that also contain the secondary staircases. These columns work as integrated parts of the space. Their different colours help to avoid things being too static. The idea is that the space will be continuously changing. There are dots of bright colours throughout the space, which act like points of departure. We have even incorporated film projections, using different colours.

The 'drums' are part of the flexible solution in the layout. The inside space can be part of the surrounding area or be shut off to form an intimate enclosed space.

On top they have a comfortable bean bag area for teamwork and relaxation. One drum is placed in each X-zone (opposite).

MC *When I look at, and move through, this building, I feel it welcoming me. This might be because the approach you took here really does communicate through the space. I mean, there is often a distance between architect and client; the ego boosting — "This is what I have done...." At the College this doesn't seem to be the case.*

KHN I'm glad that you feel this; I hope it will be the case with the students and teachers as well. I feel great every time I come into the space. And, as I've already mentioned, this is where 3XN's new life started. You see, as far as the past goes, it isn't that I don't want to be associated with that work, it's just that I'm naturally more interested in where we are right now, and how we might evolve.

MC *The other thing about the College that is impressive is the variety of spaces within the building. Certain places put you up high, and are overwhelming; and then there are those where you feel really comfortable. In each, there is something different. Interacting with these different kinds of spaces is important to enable the students and staff to shape their own space.*

KHN Even the roof contributes to the project in this way. We still haven't secured the money to complete this part of the project, but we designed the whole thing, including a garden with glasshouses, an observatory and a green area, all providing the possibility for outdoor teaching. Along with the building's natural ventilation, this is part of the sustainable and energy-saving aspects of the College.

MC *So, you have taken sustainability and the environment into account here?*

KHN Yes, absolutely, and, of course, these are aspects that we integrate more and more along with the growing awareness and the clients' willingness to invest in this. Besides the building's natural ventilation, it is very energy efficient. I wouldn't say it is a revolutionary building in this way, but it recognises and engages with the factors that make it more sustainable.

MC *So, this is a milestone in your work, and a perfect demonstration of how architecture can influence behaviour in a sensitive way.*

KHN At Ørestad College, we have attempted to create a sort of 'comfort zone' within which to positively gear the students to freer and greater knowledge. This process was also part of what we proposed for the Salford University project in Manchester.

MC *But in the UK, the approach must have been quite different, despite the government's launch of the Building Schools for the Future programme in 2004.*

KHN It was definitely more difficult. The reason being that, in the UK, I believe, there is less comfort with dialogue. Discussions there are very tough. But the fact is, one has to have a very social approach, and a different way of thinking, and the client needs to be on this same wavelength. In the UK, it seems as though all of the negotiations are about getting the best deal, and that kind of discussion doesn't usually lead to good results. It's not about who is right and wrong, which leaves out the really important part of negotiation; that is, the concept of establishing a dialogue so as to find the best solution!

Daylight is an important factor to human well-being, as well as to reducing energy consumption from artificial lighting. But this often conflicts with the desire for reduced solar gain. A flexible solution is needed. The colourful shutters on the perimeter of the Ørestad College not only allow for a flexible adjustment between daylight and sun-generated heat, they also dominate the exterior expression of the College, as well as the interior environment.

choreography

In the Lisbjerg School; an elementary school for a new urban area in Århus; tools similar to those used in the Ørestad College were employed: a choreography for life during the day aimed at creating synergy and knowledge-sharing. Competition model (this and opposite page).

MC *The principal idea that was explored at Salford, if I am not mistaken, was the integration of creative knowledge sharing and education.*

KHN That's right. Studios and other spaces are interwoven throughout the scheme, whilst at the same time being grouped around a central atrium lit from a glass roof. Again, the idea here was to bring together students and teachers, so that they might benefit from a real engagement with one another.

Our Alsion University project also had much to do with this. There, a university, a science park and a concert hall were brought together. The aim was to achieve some sort of synergy; it is the first time in Denmark that private research and public education have been located together. So, our idea was to choreograph life within the building given everyday situations, to make people climb down from their ivory towers and mingle with each other. This sort of interaction is essential, and I think it is an approach that can be seen in many of our projects — the Lisberg School, for example.

MC *Does this project in particular adopt the same principles we've just been discussing?*

KHN The Lisberg School was a competition we did in 2006 for a new urban development area's elementary school. The pupils have their 'home base' and their 'future base'; the idea being that in grades one to three, children are very musical, which provides a focus for the teaching and learning at this age; and from grades three to five, the emphasis is more on mathematics, and so on. So, in this way, we divided the school into three 'levels', with a common shared 'level' for circulation.

MC *How does the circulation work here? Is it similar to the College — that is, a central node?*

KHN No, it has a different structure. The classrooms and common space face onto a greater space. I mean, a distinct division between mathematics and the arts would be artificial and irrelevant. Again, it is about interaction, learning from each other in an inspirational way.

The school building is a compact, urban structure with four levels: an open, active ground floor that interacts closely with its surroundings, and above this are three boomerang-shaped floor decks.

✳ Lisbjerg School

The new Lisbjerg School in Århus has been given the role of generator and catalyst for an entire new district. The competition proposal's point of departure is therefore innovative and future-oriented on several levels. The aim has been to unite the latest organisational principles regarding the coherence between learning and space with experiences of noise and other challenges gained previously.

The school concept is three-sided in more than one way. It contains three age groups, three subject fields and has three important relationships; to the surrounding landscape, to a street, aimed at transport, and to a central street, aimed at integrating city life. The school will also have three different functions — as school, as community

centre and as parish centre related to the church. This has led to the building's triangular shape — not sharp, but relaxed and non-dogmatic, like a piece of broken glass, rounded by the sea.

The school building is a compact, urban structure with four levels: an open, active ground floor that interacts closely with its surroundings, and above this are three boomerang-shaped floor decks containing three subject fields and three home bases, one for each age group (seven–nine years, ten–12 years and 13–15 years). All floors are in direct visual and physical contact via the tall central atrium, and each floor has access to large open-air terraces.

In a didactic sense, the school concept combines the best from the

open school model as well as that of the traditional class room-based school. This means that a clear visual layout, interaction and synergy go hand in hand with the fact that the individual pupil can find comfort, contemplation and a possibility for absorption according to his or her age level.

The building contradicts a reliance on four traditional facades and establishes new ways of interacting with nature, city and district. The urban intentions play well along with the ambition for a school building where the daily exchange of knowledge and curiosity across age and subject borders broadens the horizons of both pupils and teachers.

Foreseen as the new district's landmark, the Lisbjerg School sets out its attention in several directions. It lines up towards the main street, while opening to the green fields devoted to sports and playing, and plays with the future scale and massing of adjacent buildings.

gateway

MC *What, then, differentiates it from your other projects? You often mention that you learn from prior experience, but then what does this scheme bring to your work that the other projects haven't?*

KHN It is the architectural language, it is more sophisticated, and this ties into the bigger picture, which is that of 'creative education'. Learning from each other, interacting and meeting, that is the concept informing the Ørestad College. The building's users meet and their activities are made visible. In doing so, they are inspired and learn more from each other. The other important aspect here is that of linking together different forms of education and different fields of knowledge. For example, you are taught a language not for the language itself, but to be able to solve a problem — to communicate. The implication being that such learning is much more relevant to the students.

MC *So, you never get lost in translation! Or do you?! What about the Far East, how do you perceive the situation in China? Is it really architecture's new frontier, or is it more of a jungle where anything goes, as most architects seem to depict it?*

KHN I think you have to be very careful in China, very selective both with regards to the project and the client. We are currently doing a project; Yangpu University District Gateway Building, in Shanghai. This is a competition that we won in 2004, which is now being built. The client is, I think, one of the best, a so-called 'blue-ribbon client', and so far everything has gone smoothly.

MC *Again, in this project you challenged the idea of interaction. The scheme is like a doppelganger, two towers facing each other...*

KHN The two buildings form a 'gateway' between the University Village and the Science Park. There is an ambition here to create a connection and interaction between the University scientists and students. And the towers do play with the idea of reflecting each other. They are similar, but at the same time they have small, subtle differences. This project is more about addressing a specific question, a specific situation — hence our incorporating the number eight into the facade, because of Chinese superstition that regards eight as a lucky number. We also had to redesign a feature that could be perceived as being an arrowhead — which is as unlucky to the Chinese as walking under a ladder is to us!

MC *Here again, the client really seems to be involved in establishing a dialogue, of being part of the point of departure informing the scheme. Another key project being built in Copenhagen at present, where the client was similarly influential, is the Saxo Bank.*

KHN That's true. We had many workshops with the client in the lead up to the scheme. The Saxo Bank is a 'trading bank', an online bank for people who want to trade using their investments. The business idea for Saxo was conceived about 15 years ago by two young businessmen in their 30s. It is now a worldwide system; they have branches in Barcelona, London and Singapore.

The two buildings are not identical, but similar; like crystalline snow flakes.

Each building has two elliptical openings oriented in opposite directions.

A pointy arrow shape has been carefully avoided in the facade design.

✳ Yangpu Gateway Buildings

The Yangpu Gateway Buildings are double-buildings that form the link between the University Village and The Hub Science Park campus in the Yangpu University City Central Area in Shanghai.

Silicon Valley in the United States is a reference for the new ambitious development in Shanghai. Innovative research businesses are here to connect with university scientists and students in order to fuel the new technological boom.

Two crystalline buildings form the competition-winning proposal. They are alike at first appearance, but display small distinctions at closer inspection — like snowflakes and mountain crystals. The prismatic volumes are cut back at their diagonals, and the system of various angles carefully complies with Chinese culture and tradition; for instance, in China people do not wish to walk under an arrow-head, as this is regarded as similar to walking under a ladder for a person in the West.

The buildings protrude to the south, while terracing backwards to the north. The resulting facets ensure multiple view lines in all directions, and lend a visual expression of the interaction that is aimed for in the area. Internally, in each building, the offices embrace a central atria and roof gardens. The atria open a transparent environment with a good sense of the life and action in the buildings.

The programme's demands were high. Significant architecture, challenging structure and a multi-functional concept including offices, retail, restaurants, leisure and underground parking were to be united. The client for the project is the private development company Shui On Land, with project documentation being done in cooperation with the Australian architects Hassel.

Saxo Bank is built according to Denmark's latest energy consumption regulations. One issue here is the diminishing of the glass area, with the challenge being how to create a more closed outer perimeter without falling back to yesterday's approach to office facades.

folding surfaces

The building volume is perceived as one object, wrapped in a continuous skin. This reduces the traditional effect of the floor deck division.

MC *So, did the banking system have anything to do with the conceptualisation of the project? I mean, the sort of smoothness and openness that one can read in the scheme, is this an interpretation of this innovative system?*

KHN Yes, it does pertain to this kind of banking which is more dynamic and flexible, and this is in some ways evident in the building. It is one big space, wherein you can see the entire trading floor. The design for Saxo Bank came right after that for the Ørestad College, and there are obvious similarities of ideas between these buildings, but of course the function and the site called for bespoke solutions as well. The site initially comprised four lots, and the master plan was decisive about short, slender buildings, with short gable ends. Therefore, we couldn't simply build a big box, which is why we cut into it, in an undulating way, creating 'gable ends'. We aimed at creating a seamless, continuous flow on the facades, using a set of structural elements as a 'skin'. We encountered problems here at first, as nobody could make the columns so sharp. But we resolved this when we found a Swedish firm who were able to achieve the rake of these walls.

The building consists of two U forms placed on top of each other, creating double-height spaces with single-heights along their edges. The building is topped out by a roof garden with a view over the ocean.

MC *So, here again, you are playing with the idea of folding surfaces. The treatment of the facade seems to move in various directions, like the folds of the Renault Truckland project.*

KHN Here too, asking questions formed a large part of our process. In this case, the conversation was very much directly with the client. They wanted the scheme to be one of many showrooms, so in this regard, it was a project without a context. So the dialogue with the client was one of the key elements informing our design process. The project was completely tailored to their needs, which we achieved through consultation and workshops.

MC *Have you ever gone against the client — what I mean here is, have you ever gone beyond the brief, thinking that you could propose a better solution than they might have laid ground for?*

KHN We do try to stick to the brief, but at the same time challenge it. And yes, sometimes we do go beyond the brief. That is, if it's clear that a client will receive a benefit from our doing so. And this is all based on the premise that the client be open to dialogue. Exceeding the brief just for the sake of form is ridiculous — the whole idea is to talk and understand one another. What are we doing here otherwise?! Such moves don't take architecture seriously, they are simply arrogant. First, things have to function, otherwise there is no meaning in architecture, and you are just inventing a story.

Saxo Bank directs its
central opening towards
the canal.

✳ Saxo Bank

Saxo Bank is a young dynamic Internet bank with a strong presence in online trading in global capital markets. The new head offices are situated right by a canal in Hellerup, Copenhagen, on the old brewery site of Tuborg. Saxo Bank was founded in 1992 in Denmark and counts around 850 staff members of 35 nationalities who serve customers from 115 different countries.

In spite of the fact that clients primarily meet their bank in cyber space, the physical gesture of the head office is of great importance to the bank's management. In part because of its iconographic quality, in part because of strong conviction that architecture and design play an important role when it comes to the employees' performance and dedication to the company. The Saxo Bank management has been an active and engaged client that wanted the optimal frames for the employees, and a unique and spectacular new headquarters.

The architecture has Saxo Bank's cutting edge profile as its point of departure. The lines are exploring the balance between dynamic expression and trustworthy solidity in a close dialogue with planning constraints and intentions. The building is conceived as two blocks facing their gable ends to the canal, and joined together by a retracted glass facades. The facades are carried out as double-curved glass walls, and the facade columns tilt 1 on 10.

Inside, a transparent and inspiring environment enhances the sense of team spirit. The open office floors centre round a softly shaped top-lit atrium with a winding main staircase. The main room and attraction is the Wall Street inspired Trading Floor that matches any American stock broker movie when it comes to tense action.

Open office floors are
centred around an atrium.

A slim spiral staircase is the
main vertical connection.

The built result is close
to the early renders for
the scheme. Opposite: the
Saxo Bank construction
site. Adjacent apartment
buildings are mirrored in
the glass facades.

tell
their story

storytelling

**Kim Herforth Nielsen and
Rasmus Kruse in early
discussions about the
narrative content of the
Renault Truckland project.**

MC *For you, then, architecture is also about its ability to
tell a story — the right story, that is. Clearly, architecture
is not an art detached from reality, it's a combination of
science, technology, history, anthropology... architecture
communicates through symbolism and meaning.*

KHN I agree. The challenge for us is to learn something
from what we are doing, to be involved with the
process coherently, while at the same time conveying
this to the client and the wider world. The role of
the client is really essential. And, while it is true that
one can develop a specific style, I believe that the
content should vitally inform each project. In this
sense, 'content' also includes the client's identity or
personality, which at this point becomes a part of the
style of a specific work.

MC *I think it is probably important that we make a
distinction between style and coherence. Being coherent
is more about what we discussed previously — of using
and reapplying experience, while style is about making
yourself recognisable. The risk is that architecture ends
up imposing a style before understanding the reality
of a place and project. The project you are referring
to is Renault Truckland, isn't it? And this was a direct
commission, wasn't it?*

KHN Not exactly. The client approached us to invite 3XN
to an international, limited competition for this project.
The story here is a very simple and clear one. What the
client wanted was to convey the very essence of what
Renault Trucks are about. This was a great opportunity
for 3XN, we enjoyed the fact that we were to design a
building for someone personally — even though this
someone was a whole company! We were telling their
story using architecture as a means to directly get across
their ideas. There was an aspect of branding a company
to all of this too that was very interesting. This is a very
special project for us.

truck stories

The globally familiar idea of the road map provided a conceptual basis and established a 'context' that would be meaningful in Europe as well as in Asia and South America.

MC *So, if one of your approaches is telling the story, you might be called a three-dimensional storyteller.*

KHN Or four-dimensional — I mean, a 'story in stone' tends to change meaning several times in the course of time, don't you think? It was a very complex relationship that demanded an intense dialogue between our team and the client. The project was for showrooms that could be located worldwide, so there was no real context. The issue here was that we had to invent a context, and in this sense our approach was about how to go about doing this effectively.

MC *Do you think there might be a problem, working without boundaries? I've always believed, in keeping with Venturi and Scott-Brown, that it is 'complexity and contradiction' that make good architecture. As an architect, one has to control ideas, and these should emerge from a rational effort, not just by throwing things together. They should be more organic, textural and, maybe, even create illusions!*

KHN I'm completely on your wavelength, and we have a sort of motto in our office, "opposition makes architecture". Real-life challenges spark inspiration and call for original responses. It's when a project gets exposed to real life that it actually starts to react and reassemble in a different way than the obvious geometrical starting points, and this is where it gets interesting. When a project offers new solutions to old questions. I also believe that the solutions and

innovations required due to gravity, fire rules, budgets, etc., make architecture more real and maybe more truthful than any other art.

The Renault Truck project had many parameters at play, and obviously the rather complex logistics had to be solved as well, besides our attempts to tell the story of the truck. Our efforts went into 'cleaning up' to establish a seemingly effortless, clean-cut building so focus would be on the identity and the trucks. I think we managed to do so — not in a literal way like the 'Duck' of Venturi and Scott-Brown — it is more subtle. The project seems to lack layers, and seems very straightforward, but I think that is the real beauty of it.

MC *It is a building that hides a lot of detail and complexity. I think that it does play with a lot of themes that are present in your work, but at the same time it has certain qualities that other projects lack. And then again, those are different stories. What is the story in this case?*

KHN There is actually a funny story here. When we started working on the project, we would visit Arup's, in London, quite often. On our first visit we brought a handful of bold and daring structures that elevated the trucks to various positions for exhibition, and Sophie Le-Bourva from Arup immediately asked us "Why are you putting the trucks up in the air? They don't belong there; put the trucks where they belong, on the streets and on the bridges." And, of course, she was right.

✳ Renault Truckland

Renault Truckland is the name of the French carmaker's vision for a new showroom and training facility for their truck division. This proposal is envisioned as a landmark; a landscape superstructure that encompasses the entire site, which is located in a green corridor near Lyon.

The aesthetic quality has been designed to represent the characteristics of the Renault Truck brand in a worldwide context — plans were to expand the winning design to sites in China and South America. As a consequence, and because of obvious reasons regarding the substance of the building, the design responds to the 'home of the truck'; generated from the globally familiar idea of the roadmap, it resembles highways — the true element of the truck.

The proposal develops a repetitive curvilinear morphology that can be adapted and moulded to Truckland's variety of places, spaces and functions; to orient itself to the various directions of access, and to embrace a complex series of concerns into a seamless, integrated whole.

A scissor-section connects ground floor and roof into a continuous field. Three sequences of curvilinear plates — like giant slides — rise from the landscape as well as from within the structure. They meet and create access up and down. Inside, this is the 'truck playground' where topography creates opportunities to display trucks at different angles and heights, demonstrating their agility and making them visible from all points of the hall.

The reception area is the focal point where a guest will be surrounded by showrooms, theme spaces, a truckers' cafe and an amphitheatre, all situated in a diversified yet functionally coherent and visible space.

The proposal stood alone in the final, but Renault ended up — in spite of huge enthusiasm — worrying that 3XN's edifice was too specialised, and difficult to sell for other purposes, and abandoned this initial winning scheme.

Preliminary design is an iterative process — some initial reference points were a 3-D expression of the brief's requirements, set up against formal exercises in foam board models.

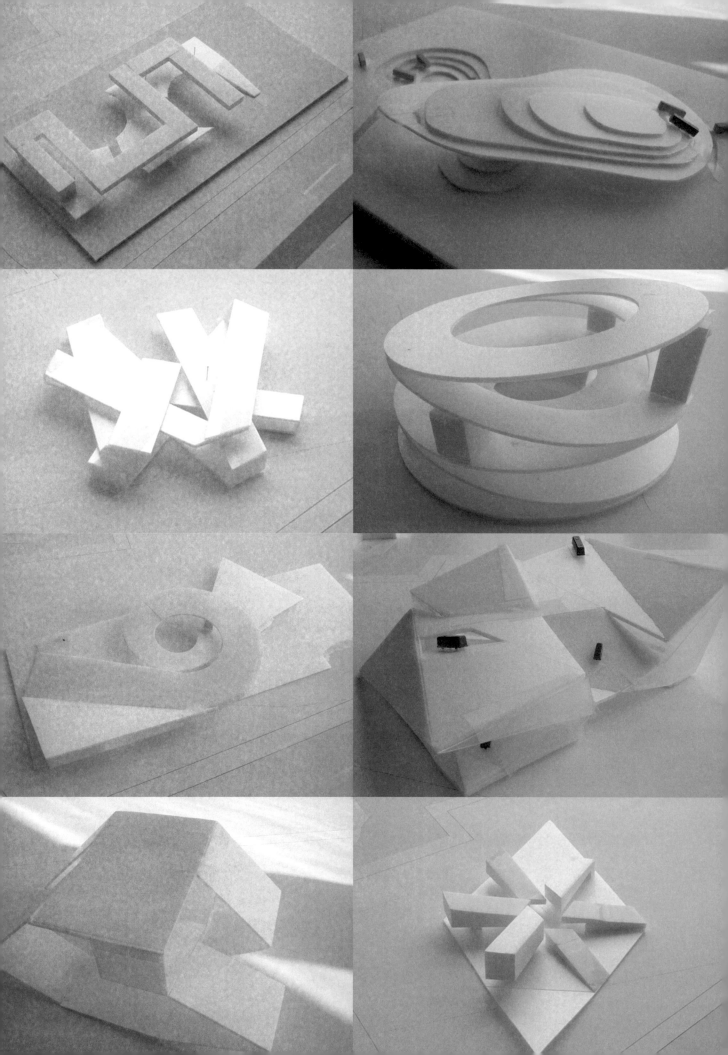

One first attempt narrowed in on a sort of fluid landscape that provided a 'playground' for the trucks exhibited.

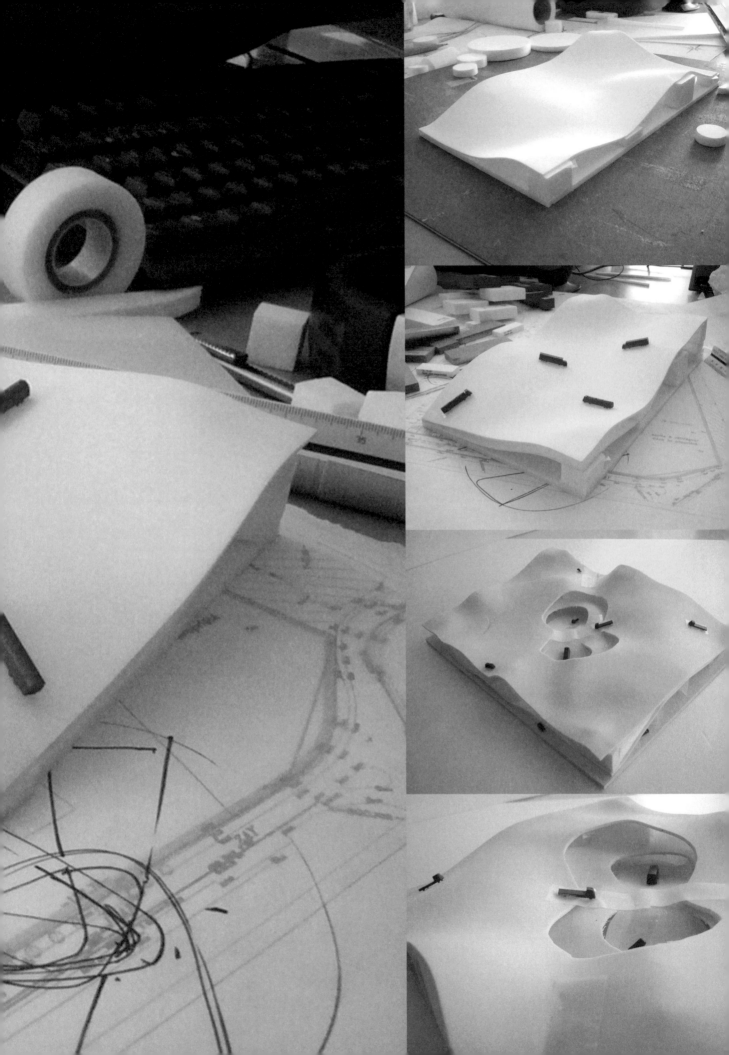

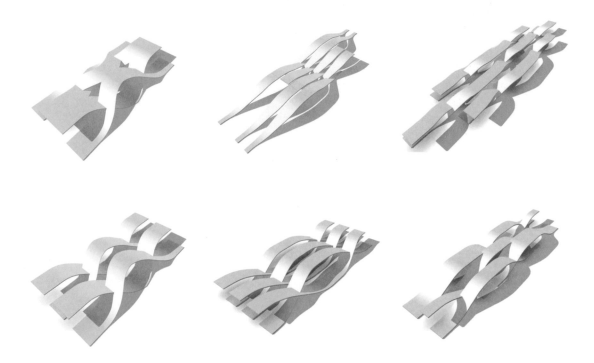

Preliminary sketches of road-like strips, woven together to form a building structure.

Conceptual model: the 'true element' of the truck is the highway.

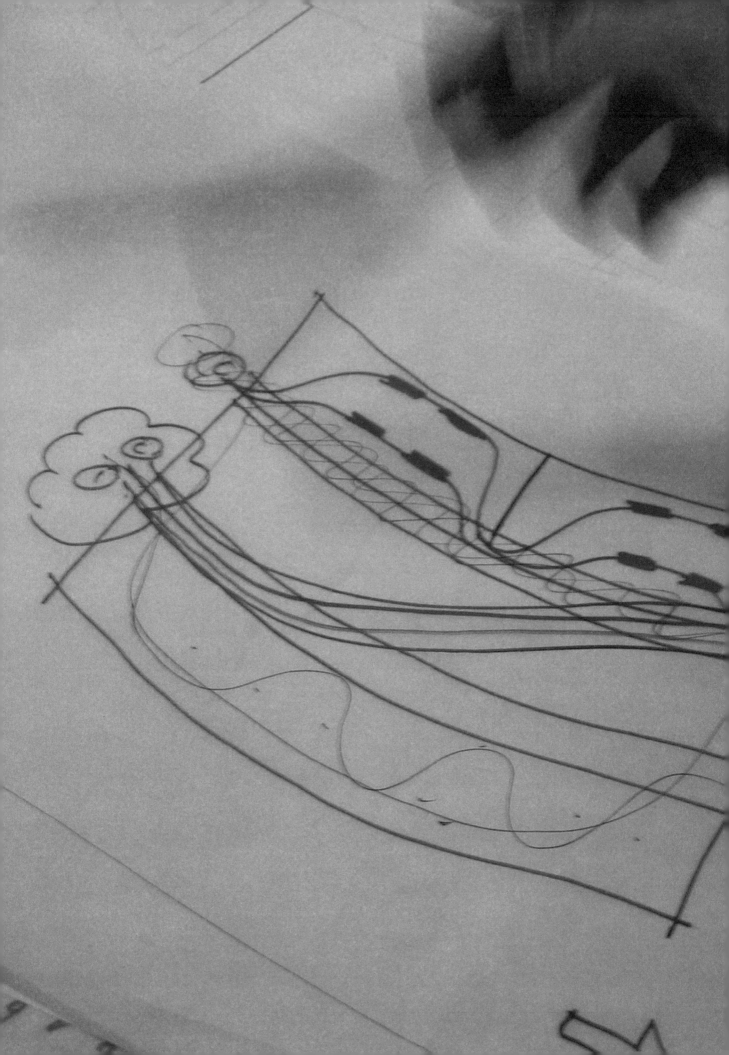

unfolding topography

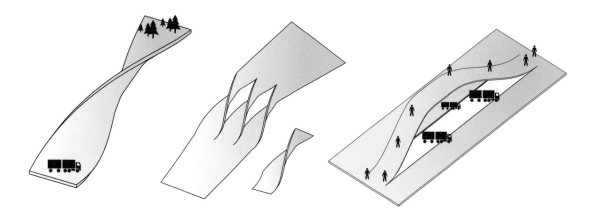

**Surface is transformed
into a spatial structure by
cutting and interweaving
landscape and building
strips. This combines the
desire for topography with
the notion of roads and
highways as a truck's true
surroundings.**

MC *From the first stages of the scheme it looked like you
move from structures to a sort of figure-ground dialectic.*
KHN Originally, we went for a topographical project, but
we tried out some more elaborate structures. Once we'd
spoken to Sophie, though, we were sure that we were
not telling the right story. The true home of the trucks
is roads. So we went back to our initial thoughts and we
started creating a structured landscape, literally playing
with trucks and roads. We carried out research into
actual motorways and motorway engineering, and that's
how we came up with the smooth, curvilinear shapes.
From here, we started interweaving the roads and
green areas into the building. The proposal developed
a repetitive morphology that was able to adapt and
mould itself to a variety of sites, because one of many
parameters was to consider a replication of the project to
other sites than the actual one in Lyons. China and Brazil
were mentioned as other possibilities. Our response to
this 'lack of context' was to consider the roadmap as
a global familiarity, and that the true elements of the
truck are highways, parking lots and so on, with their
typological characteristics. We built various models
and explored surface relations until we came up with a
structure that framed all demands, and was very clear.
I actually like this story very much because it tells how
we tackled a specific problem and resolved it, and in this
case the whole building tells the story.

This working model provided answers to several concerns: how to integrate planning demands for interacting with a 'green corridor' in the area; how to create a challenging topographic exhibition area for the trucks; and how to transform a 2-D flat landscape, using cutting and slicing as a modelling strategy, into a 3-D structure that opens and provides internal space (see also overleaf).

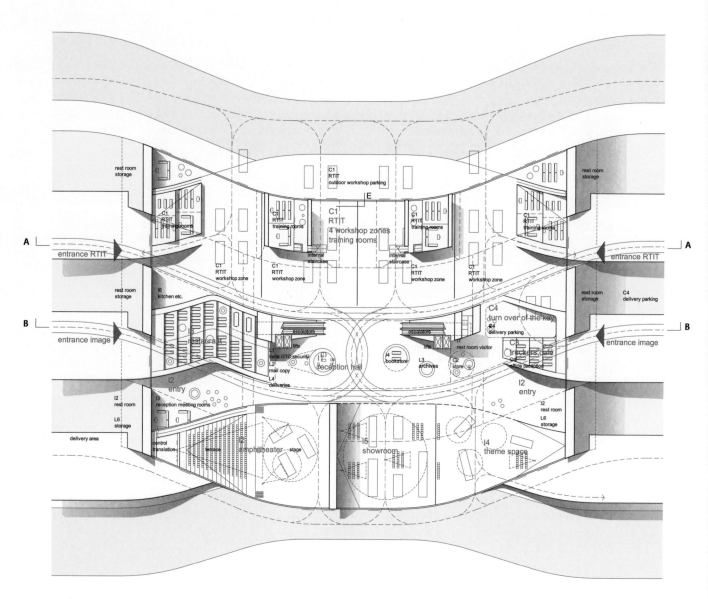

Level 1 | 1:1000

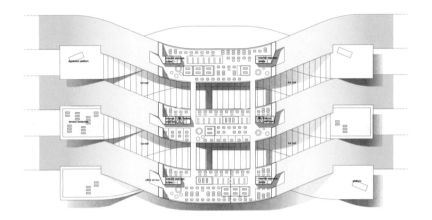

Level 3 | 1:2000

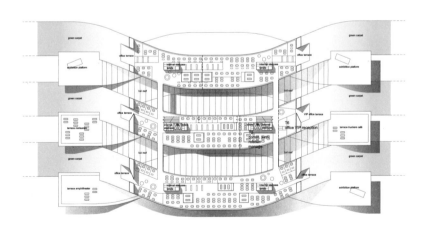

Level 2 | 1:2000

Research into highway
design and structural
bridge engineering
inspired the smooth,
curvilinear shapes.

North elevation | no scale

East elevation | no scale

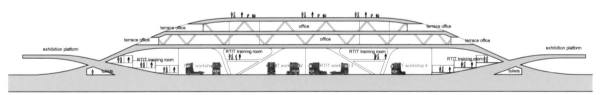

Section AA | no scale

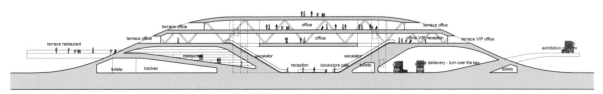

Section BB | no scale

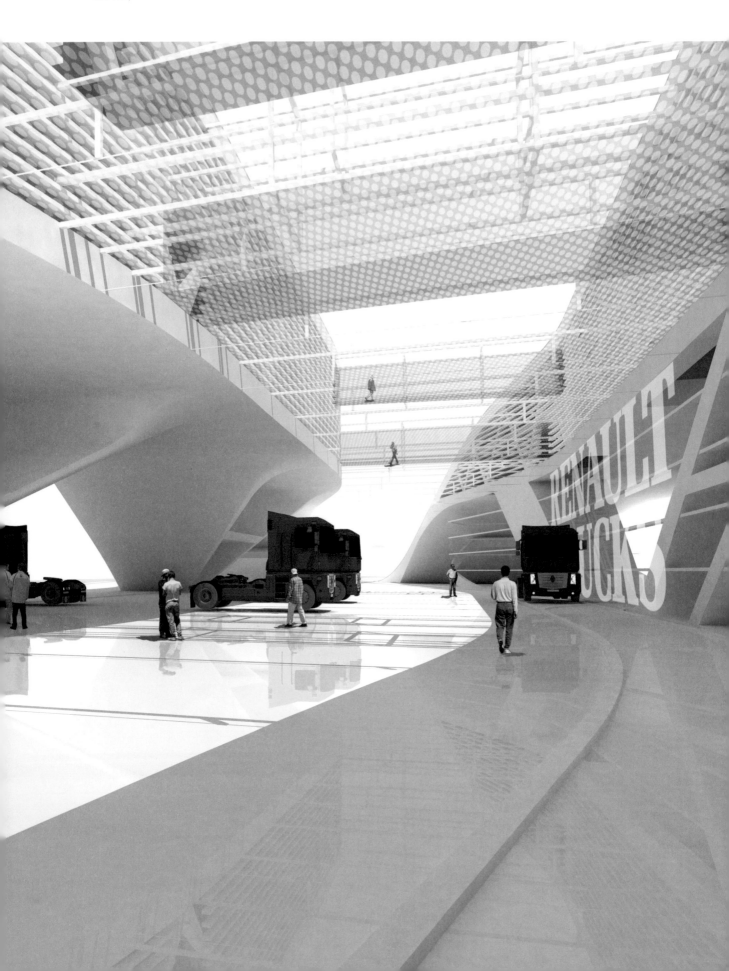

particular universality

 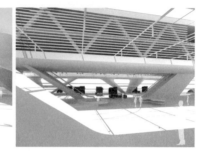

**Spaces designed to convey
a specific identity may,
in time, also serve other
purposes without loosing
functionality. But would
the loss of story (the truck),
then, negatively influence
the spatial experience?**

MC *You passed the first stage with great success and
applause and went on to the second stage, just 3XN
and a French architect. Here, you were faced with the
question "What if Renault Trucks wants to sell the
buildings to a completely different client at a later
stage?" This sounds absurd, especially as the client was
asking for something iconic and brand-building?*

KHN Yes, that's true, it was a difficult question since
we had put a lot of emphasis on Renault Trucks and
their specific identity. But in the end, we thought that
what we were proposing had also a generic aspect, and
was something that could be seen along any highway.
We had done a scissor-section that connected the
ground and roof of the building into a continuous
field. There were access points on both floors, and this
kind of topography created various spaces that could
be used for exhibitions, showrooms, a cafe and even
an amphitheatre. All of these were situated in diverse
yet coherent spaces, and all of them were, in some way,
geared to Renault's identity — but could also have been
used for other purposes.

MC *But something went wrong! Was it that they didn't
buy into the story, or they didn't want that particular
story, or was it more political?*

KHN They loved the story — all the design directors there
were crazy about the project, they loved it. Even the
public relations manager expressed his enthusiasm
— and after all, it is his job to know what effectively
brands Renault Trucks. What they told us was that it
was down to the economics of the project, and that the
president of Renault had played a key role.

MC *I also think that people don't buy stories any more.
I mean, we are living, more and more, in an era of
responsibility. It's like we are standing on the edge of
a cliff. Architecture is about thinking and, in a certain
way, about slowness — it needs time. Today, computers
make everything fast. And while computers are essential
tools that optimise time, structure and form, you may
sometimes find yourself pushing a button and a thing
acquires a life of its own.*

KHN I agree. People don't take the time anymore to
tell or even think of stories — and by stories I mean
concepts. For example, I believe it was the story we
told with our building in Liverpool that made the
difference. It was the story of Liverpool, seen on
different levels and through different layers, but it was
all in relation to Liverpool's historical background and
its projected desires for the future.

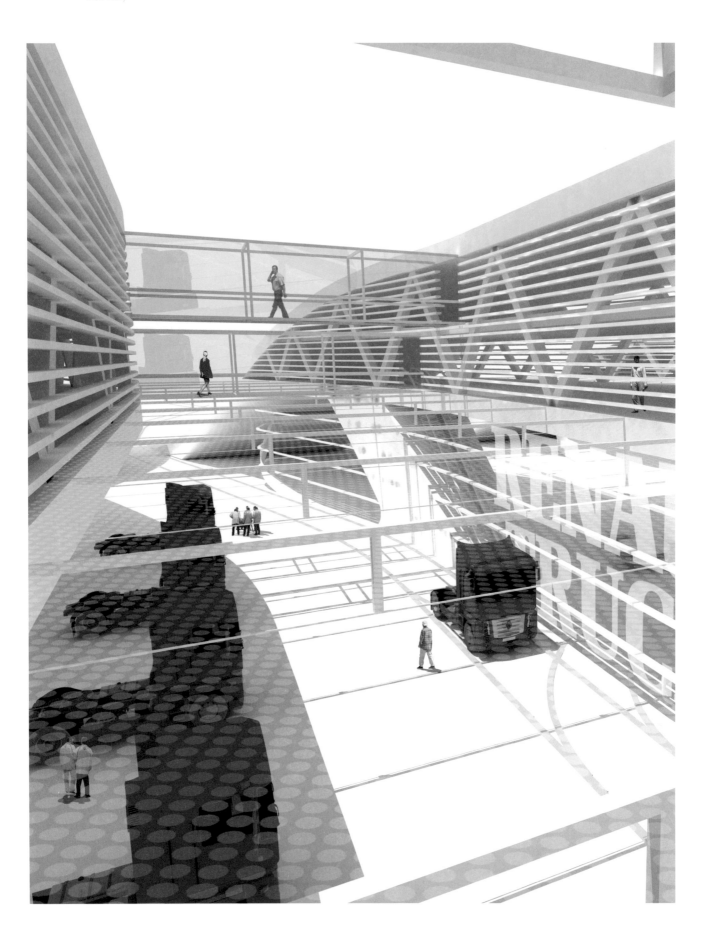

contradiction

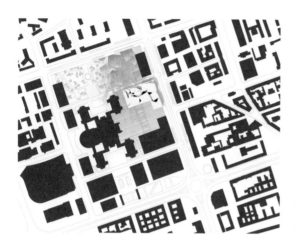

**Museum of Modern Art,
Warsaw, Poland; site.
Telling a story sometimes
also means making a stand
and confronting old legends
with tales of the present.**

MC *And it wasn't just a story about the city, but also about how to read a museum. The Museum of Modern Art in Warsaw is another such project, isn't it?*

KHN It's about the current situation in Poland. The country has changed from a dictatorship to becoming more of a Western democracy, and is starting to establish itself within the European community. The idea, therefore, was to build an icon that would help revitalise the city. The project has to do with several issues, from cultural aspects of the Museum itself, to master planning. It is next to the cultural building, which was commissioned by Stalin, and 'handed away' to the Polish people in such a way that they had to pay for it!

MC *So did that influence the design?*

KHN It did — because even the masterplan enhances the old Stalinist monument. It is a very strong fascist building, and we knew that our idea for the Museum really had to act as a counterpart to this building and play against it. The entire concept for our project was a protest, a protest against a formalistic way of thinking. Our design appears chaotic, in the sense that it is doing just the opposite of the formalistic building. It is more of an anarchist-like statement — in a positive sense. The edges of it are cut off, it is like a person who is trying to reach out but is cut off.

MC *I think this is also one of the building's strengths,*

because it plays in a significant way with its materiality, which I think has to evolve out of the culture and the place.

KHN On the one hand, the Museum is related to this city, and builds on this context as a result of its position; but on the other hand, it provides you with the opportunity to go up against the Stalinist building. It is also a question of designing a piece of city, not just a building. The solution, I think, was very appropriate for the actual situation, since it emphasised the importance of the place, and to do that, one has to create a theoretical background or a research background.

MC *I am reminded of Calatrava, who said, to paraphrase, that design is not only the will of a single person, but more like a religious idea, like binding things together. What better example here than that of your hometown of Århus. There, you were able to tell a story with the Lighthouse project.*

KHN You just can't simply place an object; it's more about absorbing and interpreting. The Lighthouse had a lot to do with that, because Ben van Berkel and I wanted to tell the story about Århus, about how it is a city by the water and how one really experiences it. When I first came to Århus to start my education as an architect, I would always go the waterfront to watch the sea, and in some way that was an inspirational factor that was built into the project.

The entire concept was a protest against a formalistic way of thinking. The design appears chaotic, doing just the opposite of the Stalinist building.

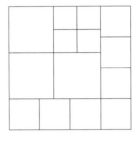

Brief

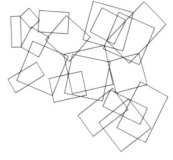

Composition

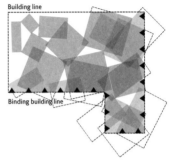

Cut by building regulations

✱ The Museum of Modern Art in Warsaw

Art is the spark that is struck when work and the ambient world meet. This concept forms the basis for the proposal for Warsaw's new Museum of Modern Art — its very essence is the vibrant interface between the building and the city. The Museum's concept is the juxtaposition of the inner rationale of the Museum and the intrinsic order and nature of the surrounding city and park. Two very different ambiences; the soft, natural verdancy of the park juxtaposed to the precise, representative lines of the city, not least symbolised by the Palace of Culture and Science ('given' to Warsaw by Stalin) and the city's severe, symmetrical layout.

The basic architectural unit is the rectangular box — the ideal space for the presentation of art. Add rectangular box to rectangular box and you have a museum. The Museum consists of eight rectangular exhibition boxes of various sizes, offset from each other horizontally and vertically. A number of smaller boxes containing the foyer, the educational centre, etc., complement the larger exhibition boxes.

Vertically, spaces are not just separated by walls as in traditional architecture — each individual box is a completely separate unit placed at varying angles from the other boxes.

This creates voids and gaps between the boxes. The complex of boxes forms a dynamic totality full of movement, while each box in itself emanates absorption and contemplation.

The gaps admit daylight and allow the visitor glimpses of the ambient world. This serves as a reminder of the world outside and — more pragmatically — as an aid to general orientation. The gaps form links between exhibition spaces and act as psychological breathing spaces between one absorbing art experience and the next.

Daylight access and internal visual connections occur in the intermediate spaces, which are as important to the project as the exhibition boxes.

level 6
level 5
level 4

Section AA | no scale

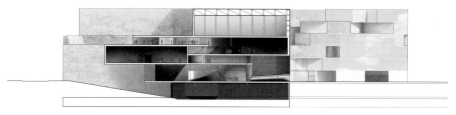

Section BB | no scale

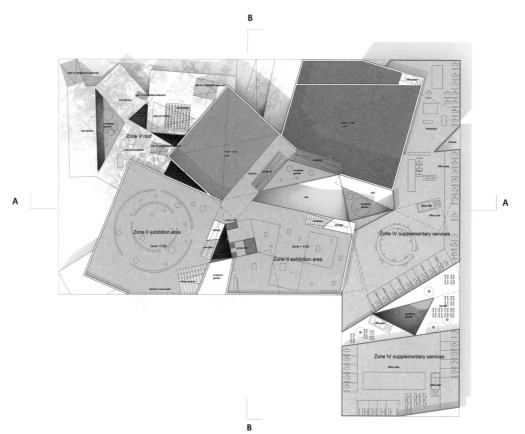

Plan level 4 | no scale

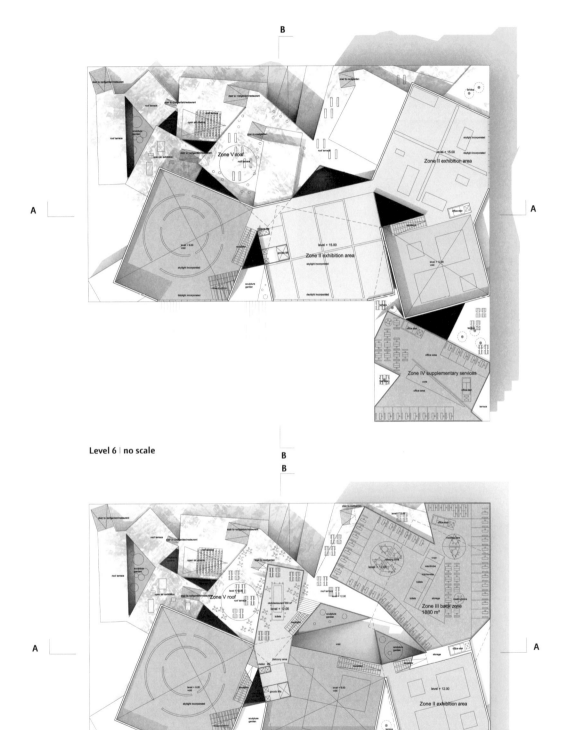

Level 6 | no scale

Level 5 | no scale

**Oceanarium. Large tank
windows offer the public
an experience of the North
Sea underwater world.**

Once you move an element close to another, you create a third; the space in-between.

MC *Speaking of the sea as an inspiration, didn't you build the world's largest coldwater aquarium?*
KHN We did, it was about eight years ago, the Oceanarium. The story to tell there is that it imitates the harsh environment of the North Sea. And, with its 4.5 million litres of 14 degree salt water, it's like you said, the largest coldwater aquarium in the world.
MC *What was the inspiration for it?*
KHN In the brief, the client wanted a huge aquarium tank where large audiences would be able to look into it simultaneously at different angles, yet not be able to see each other. The idea here was that, with these huge glass window panels the viewer would be provided with the sensation of looking into a never-ending ocean.
MC *This kind of inspiration — from the sea — has informed your work throughout the years. Another project in this context is the House of Architects in Copenhagen.*

KHN The story behind that project is it's location in an old area of the city, where the old dockyards used to be. We played with this context. The building is conceived as three elements: one is the concrete block towards the street, the other the wooden shrine towards the harbour, with a staircase in-between, and all framed by a glass box. Initially, I wanted to open up the entire old dock, but the state couldn't provide the money for it, so in the end we made a modest waterfall as a reference or symbol, and played with the effects of this outside the building. This project is about telling the story and history of the site and the surrounding docks.
MC *This is an important project, as it brings up another discourse that runs throughout several of your projects; that of a void between two elements.*
KHN Well, in this project we can clearly see that the two elements are separated by a tall slim room, with

the steel grid carrying the staircase, elevators and footbridge. This is an architectural language that is very important to us. Once you move two elements close to each other, you start creating a third — the space in-between.

MC *And there are references here to the Music Building.*

KHN Actually, that was the lead concept for it. The story there was that we had to provide new common premises for two well-established institutions, the Ijsbreker and the Bimhuis. By installing a wide staircase, we played with the idea of connecting these elements with the pier and the water, while creating a spectacular access route through the interior.

MC *This is a very successful project, but the Royal Danish Embassy, 1999, was clearly a predecessor for this concept. In that building, the void is very strong and is actually what gives the building its identity.*

KHN True. The Royal Danish Embassy was a precedent for the Music Building, while, at the same time, it was resting on our experiences from the Architects' House. Looking at the Embassy from the outside, it seems like one building, but once inside it is revealed as a complex of buildings.

MC *It creates a feeling that, behind the semi-transparent facade, there is a microcosm, a city within a city, where light enters through unexpected openings, and where public and private spaces are juxtaposed to create a whole.*

KHN The idea here was about our trying to tell a particularly Danish story, where tradition and history blend harmoniously with technology. Light, in this sense, was very important, and I think that our contribution to the scheme is the most well lit of all of the Embassy buildings in the Nordic Complex. The other important aspect here was that of materials. As you were saying, the building consists of two separate volumes, one undulating, soft and 'warm', the other sharp, 'cold' and prismatic.

MC *Was that also dictated by the brief? I mean, certain parts of an embassy are required to be private and secure, while others are to be more open to the public.*

KHN The embassy complex as a whole is very secure. For simple affairs, people only use the common building outside the 'fence'. Inside the Danish Embassy, the two volumes are connected by a hall space, which is a four-storey tall glass covered foyer, with a cross pattern of walkways that link the buildings together. These walkways have come to be used for confidential conversations. You will see this scheme in many of our buildings — we like to use staircases as meeting spaces.

MC *Yes, like in the Ørestad College.*

KHN Exactly! In the Embassy, the 'curved' volume follows the louvered organic form characteristic of the entire complex, while the curved ash wooden louvered wall is tapered inwards, towards the top, creating a sharper tension between the two 'heavy' volumes. The broad opening in the Embassy, topped by a balcony bearing the Danish coat of arms, is instead an inviting entrance to the front hall and reception area from the complex's inner plaza. Looking back now, I think this really was a predecessor to many of our projects, and from it emerges a number of the themes that have subsequently run throughout our practice.

**The House of Architects.
The intermediate space.**

**The House of Architects.
A lantern towards the
harbour.**

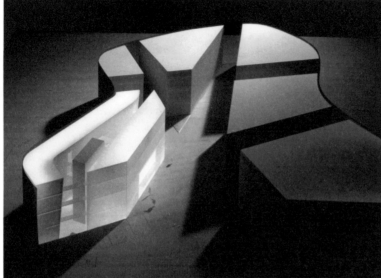

The Royal Danish Embassy
forms part of the Nordic
Embassy Complex in
Berlin, together with,
from clockwise above,
Iceland, Norway, Sweden
and Finland. The lower
right element is the
common building.

✳ The Royal Danish Embassy

The Danish Embassy in Berlin is a part
of the Nordic Embassy Complex, which
is framed by a sweeping copper band.
This copper band, along with all outer
boundaries, was set in a previous
masterplan competition.

The concept basically consists of a
parallel shifting of the two long sides
of the scheme inwards, to establish a
double-shape, which is separated by a
tall glass-roofed panoptical area. One
element moves punctually along the
curved lines of the copper band, which
emphatically marks its imprint on the
inner area. The second element creates
a certain tension with its double, being
prismatic and clear-cut.

The contrasts in shape are followed
in the materials used. Inside the lobby,
a transparent screen of wooden louvers
runs parallel to the undulating element
of the building, recapturing — the only
one of the five Embassy buildings — the
external shape of the complex. The
'soft' wooden screen is set off against
the prismatic element facing the inner
plaza. This volume is clad in perforated
steel sheets, inside as well as out — to
indicate the volume as an entity.

The conspicuous wooden screen
is a piece of precision work, with its
long louvres in ash wood, the innate
strength of which is well suited for the
long, straight spans. The veins in ash

further lend structure and character
to the louvres without disturbing the
impression of brightness.

Due to the inward tilt of the wooden
screen, the lobby becomes narrower
upwards. This intensifies the tension in
the 'gorge' between the two buildings,
and, on a more practical level, increases
space along with the elevation and
importance of the offices.

The lobby is criss-crossed by bridges,
enabling the users to experience the
open four floors of the building, and to
maintain an impression of the on-going
life in the building.

doppelganger

**The two towers of the Bella
Hotels stand as a pair.**

MC *Yes, if we follow up on the concept of the void and the
two entities, we are led to the idea of the doppelganger
in your work. Here, I am thinking about the Bella Centre
in Copenhagen.*

KHN The Bella Centre is an old trade fair complex
located between the old city centre and Ørestad. They
have long needed hotel accommodation, and they asked
us to work both on the master planning of a new trade
fair centre and on a new landmark hotel of 800 rooms.
And you are right, the two towers stand close to one
another as a pair, and they create a tension between
themselves, but they incline in opposite directions.
The reason for this was partly because of the brief and
partly to tell the story. Here, they were used as signage
and could only be the height that they are due to the
restrictions given the airport nearby. The top twist is for
wind factors, the bottom is to indicate the entrance.

MC *What is also interesting is that they are both very
slim, providing all the rooms with clear views. The
other thing that I think is very present in your work,
and that we should point out, is the way you dealt with
the facade. I think it is one of the underlying themes in
3XN's work.*

KHN Well, it's the idea of following a project through to
the last detail. I believe that one of the key qualities of
being an architect is not only the art of telling the story,
but an ability to build this story.

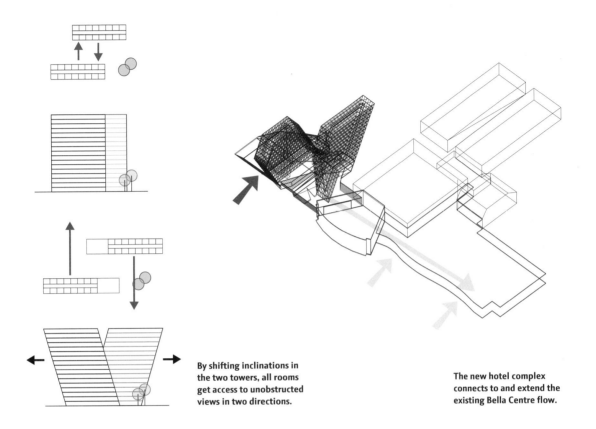

By shifting inclinations in the two towers, all rooms get access to unobstructed views in two directions.

The new hotel complex connects to and extend the existing Bella Centre flow.

✳ Bella Hotels

A new landmark hotel and conference centre is first step of the long-anticipated extension of the Bella Centre; Copenhagen's famous Congress Centre. The upgrade of the Bella Centre will add an urban feeling to the place, and the extension will immediately benefit from the Bella Centre's perfect location: situated between the old city core and Ørestad, Copenhagen's centre of growth. The Bella Centre is connected to two important worlds of activity, and furthermore, it's close to the Metro, as well as Copenhagen Airport.

Initially, 3XN worked out a masterplan for the entire Bella Centre area to establish the right place for the two-tower hotel. The masterplan is flexible and may be executed in several phases. It draws upon the classical urban weave of rectangular streets and blocks, but leaves each field open to interpretation.

The two hotel towers stand close as a pair, yet seem a little shy; the towers incline in opposite directions. The reason for this is to obtain an unobstructed view from all rooms in each tower of the surrounding flat landscape. The sky was not the limit in this case; flight safety requires a maximum tower height of 75 metres (25 floors) this close to the airport, so one tall tower was not an option.

Wind considerations, as well as the desire for a landmark building, caused the top twist of one tower, while the requirement for a clearly indicated entrance led to the ground floor twist of the other tower. The hotel lobby merges into the existing entrance lobby of the Bella Centre, making the hotel a truely integrated part of the larger scale, ready for large events, like the Copenhagen International Fashion Fair — this time with rooms for rent.

draw

the detail

under the roof

Sometimes, one single detail sums up the essence of a building. In the Middelfart Savings Bank, the concept depends on the large roof to be transparent to daylight and views, which again depends on the parallelogram-shaped 'attic'. Detailing this in the right way is therefore essential.

MC *We discussed earlier how attention to detail can bring a special quality to a project — Mies said "God is in the details"! Architecture is currently preoccupied with frivolous shapes, pattern-making and decoration. It is important, therefore, to avoid interpreting your work in these terms. Your concern for the architectural detail is a powerful statement that is apparent throughout your work. It's not only visible in the interiors but also on the external fabric of your buildings, and this is what gives cohesion to the work. It is, evidently, a point of departure. And it's also a process that is continually in flux.*

KHN The more you draw the more you know, and as a result you can integrate and experiment. That is why we set up a group in our office that carries out research in this area.

MC *I believe that the Middelfart Savings Bank project relies on this approach — and is still in development.*

KHN The Middelfart Savings Bank was interesting, in part, as we initially met the client in Liverpool. It was a competition for a new head office that had to integrate their existing building. When we first met, we asked if there was any chance of making major changes to the existing building, possibly even demolishing it. They rejected these ideas and insisted that it remain in its current state. In the end, we decided to use the old building and extended the roof of the new addition to cover it. This simple concept, gathering everything under one roof, was the idea that won us the competition.

✳ Middelfart Savings Bank

The Middelfart Savings Bank's new head office satisfies the Savings Bank's high ambitions on many levels. Internally, the building ensures an interactive and open working environment. As one of the first developments along the harbour front, the architecture positively stresses demands for a high quality future. Given the small-scale urban situation, the building installs itself harmoniously into its environment; and yet it points out that the Savings Bank is a front runner architecturally and technically, which in turn reflects the Bank's core values regarding banking business.

A terraced interior creates visibility between the different work places on different levels and integrates existing building reminiscences to the north. The Savings Bank's 'facilities' include a cafe, a book shop, a real estate agent and a fashion shop, all situated around an internal central square.

This internal layout is covered by one large plane; a filigree structure with numerous openings, designed to emphasise the transparent organisation of the Bank by bringing in abundant amounts of daylight and allowing for a direct view to the water and the Little Belt Bridge from anywhere inside the building.

In this way, the light and friendly atmosphere sought by the Bank is achieved, while still exploiting the site's potential to the extreme — it is a very deep building, with a relatively high floor/plot ratio.

The building is a pilot project for thermo-active constructions. A heating/cooling system, which stores the night's cool air and releases this during the day, is installed inside the concrete floor deck and roof elements and helps in energy saving.

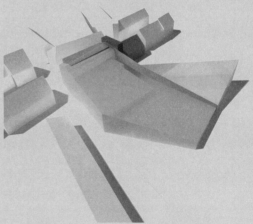

The building spans an entire block, from the picturesque shopping street to the harbour front. This diagram shows the existing building structures (red and green) that had to be incorporated into the project.

site

Middelfart is a small-scale provincial town with a two-storey pedestrian street, Algade, as its centre (top left). It is situated by the Little Belt; the waters between Jutland and Funen. Algade is connected to Havnegade (Harbour Street) via several small streets, all with a view to the sea (centre right).
A new cultural centre (centre left) is intended to catalyse harbour promenade development, to which the Savings Bank will contribute substantially. From many locations, the Little Belt Bridge (1970) is a dominating landmark, and an important part of Middelfart's identity (bottom right).

MC *I think, though, that the strength of the idea lies in how the form of the roof relates to the site, and particularly the quality of the detailing.*

KHN That's absolutely true, and if you look at it, the idea was to give a view of the ocean from inside the building, while also providing protection from the sun. So the form has a clear function, it is not an arbitrary shape. The client also requested a huge space that would serve as a covered plaza for the city, for instance a place to gather for the traditional Christmas tree party.

MC *Although that might sound strange, you mentioned that this was a small town savings bank, and that it also functioned as a community building.*

KHN Well yes, because the Bank is the centre of this area, and clearly a social space for the community. They wanted to contribute to the city in this way. For us, it was important to create a space that could be like an internal plaza that would lead to a variety of spaces: a bookshop and cafe, a real estate office and, obviously, the functions of the Savings Bank. The rest of the Bank is organised around the plaza on a series of terraces

that are linked by spacious staircases that provide the opportunity for informal meetings.

MC *But what I think is the most important aspect of the roof, is that it functions in a variety of ways. It's not only a roof, it maintains a dialogue with the site, and provides a cultural narrative.*

KHN Absolutely, and that's why we had to get it right! It's also a sustainable project. Not only does it have natural ventilation, but it also uses thermal active flooring. The mass, weight and storage capacity of the huge concrete decks is used in this way. They are bonded together with channels so that air or water can pass through them to heat or cool the building.

MC *Yes, so in this case, it is the detailing of the entire building that is important. You also chose to involve Olafur Eliasson in this project.*

KHN We did, and that fulfilled the client's requirement of dedicating one per cent of the budget to an artist. Since we are friends and had already worked together, we proposed him to the client, successfully.

Site plan | no scale

One of the ideas behind
the large roof and its
construction was to
establish a view to the
Little Belt Bridge from
all locations within
the building.

To ensure maximum
transparency in physical
and organisational terms,
the layout of the Bank is
terraced with open decks
at different heights. Most
working areas and client
contact spaces are placed
here, while the secondary
functions such as archives,
libraries and short-term
offices are placed towards
Algade, in the covered areas.

At ground floor level
a large plaza unites the
Bank's cashier desks with
a cafe, a fashion shop and
a real estate agent. The
plaza has an indoor and an
outdoor section; seamlessly
connected with natural
stone paving (opposite).

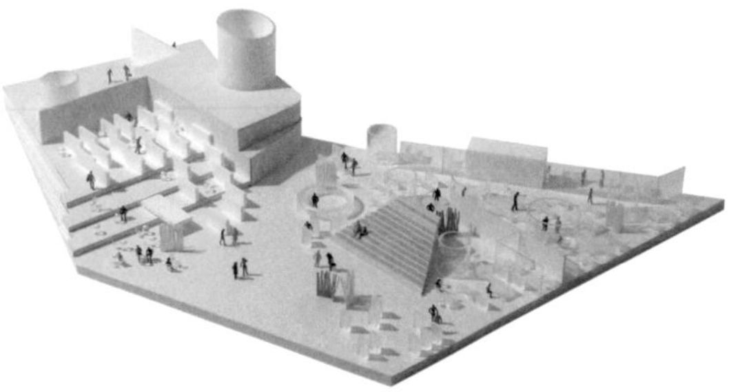

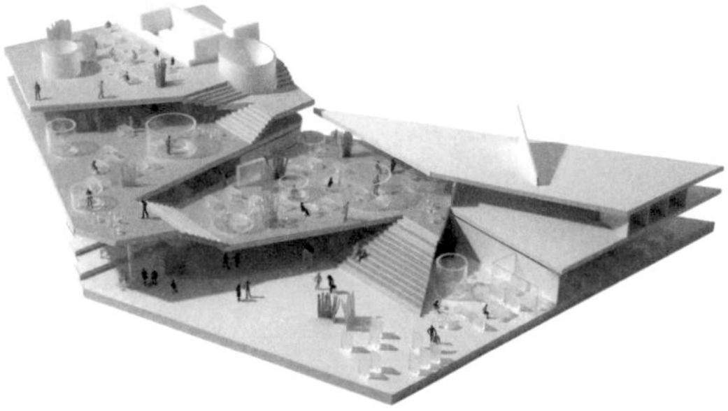

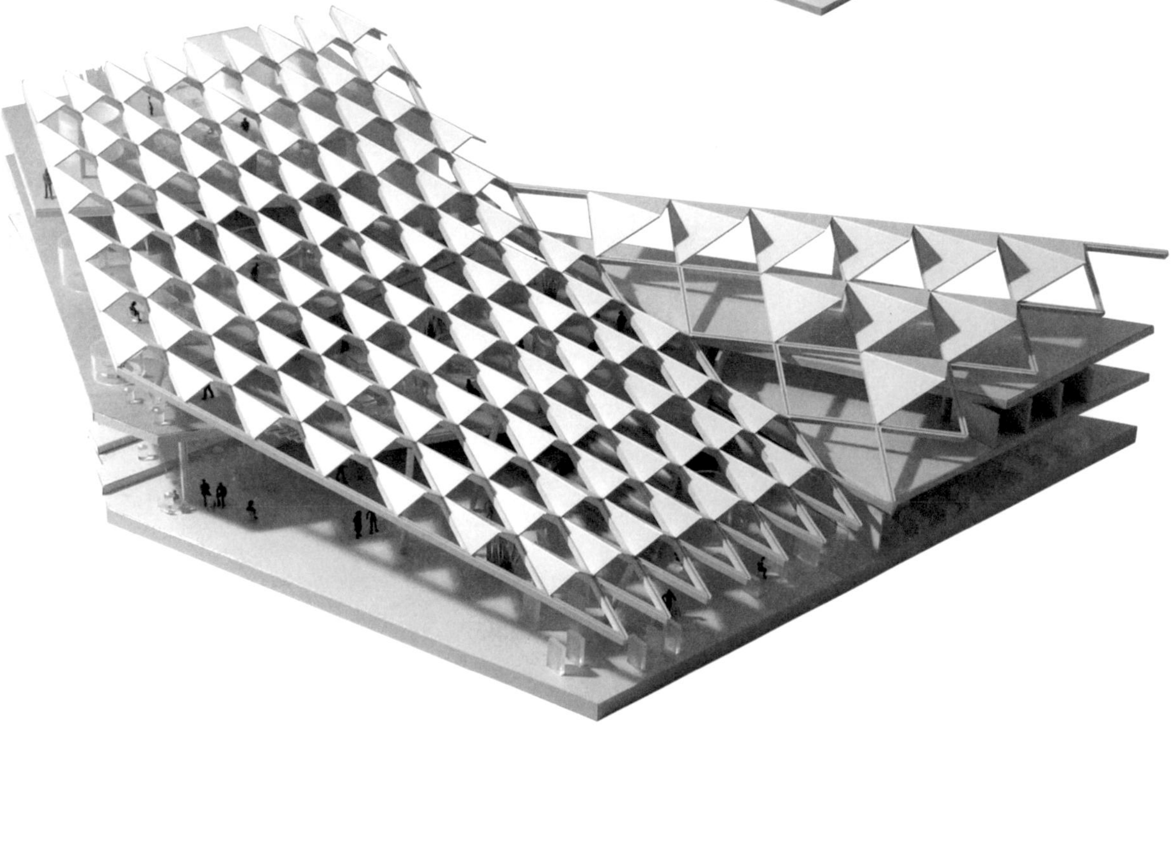

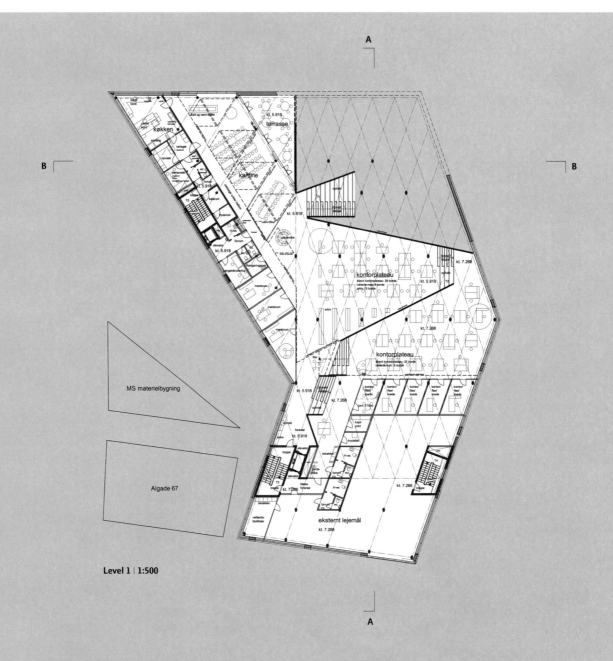

Level 1 | 1:500

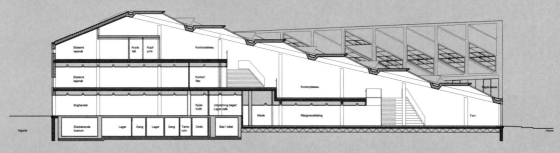

Section AA | 1:500

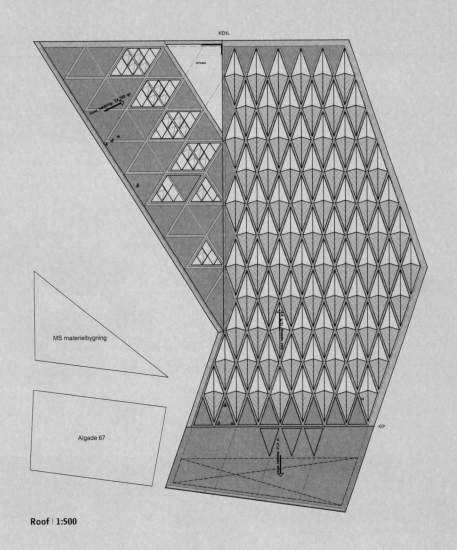

Roof | 1:500

Section BB | 1:500

light, views and air

Concept: a traditional vertical facade would be too imposing on the small-scale harbour front, and would have limited the view to the outside for those office areas near the facade.

By diminishing the harbour side facade and tilting the roof, good views from deep inside the building are also achieved, especially when combined with the terraced layout.

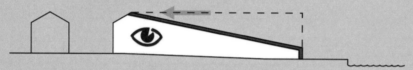

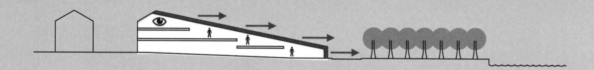

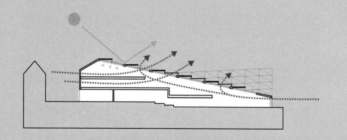

The 'multiple attic' construction not only opens to views to the outside, it also enables the extended use of natural ventilation in the building. Renderings are used for investigating the relationships between construction thickness and the building's openings (opposite).

The importance of the roof
construction details led to
several model trials. This
model is at a scale of 1:20
and was used to decide
the rational geometry that
makes the construction
affordable and buildable.

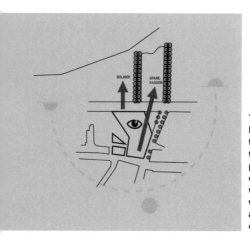

The orientation of the building is optimum: the fine view to the sea is to the north, making it possible to have large openings towards the view without having problems with solar heating and, as a result, high energy consumption for cooling.

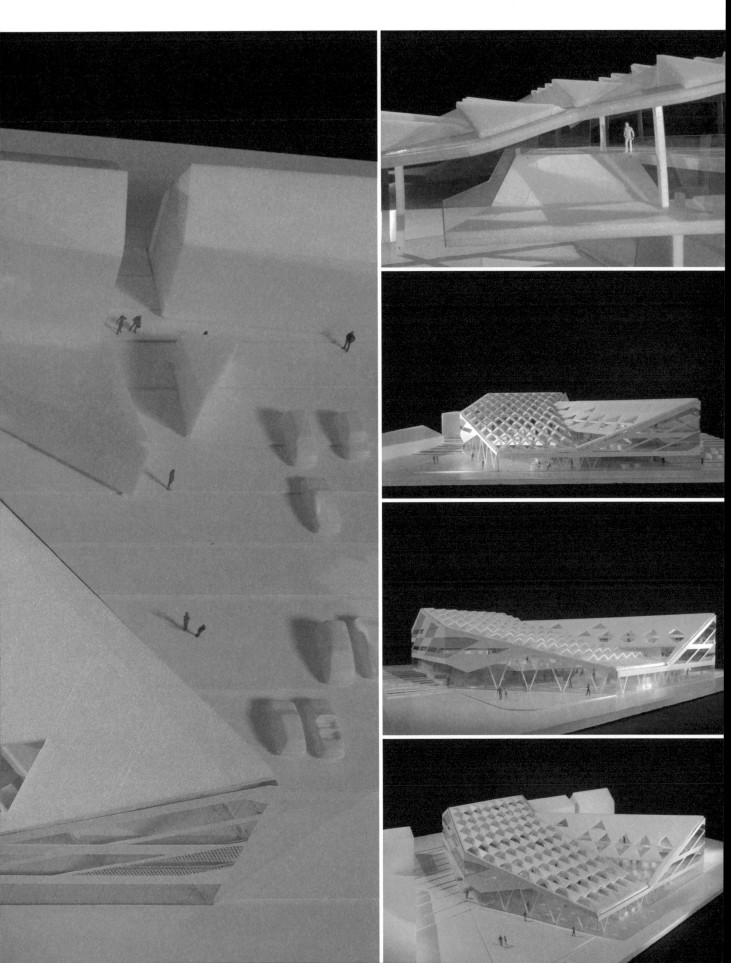

flexibility

Alsion is situated by the water in Sønderborg, a relatively small town in Denmark. Efforts have been made to scale down the building complex in relation to its context.

By dividing the building complex into a series of elements with short gable ends (opposite), the complex corresponds to the heterogenic formal language of the harbour front across the water from the University (below).

MC *Are you referring to Alsion, the mixed university, science park and concert hall?*

KHN That's when we started working together. Alsion was a competition for a relatively large university and science park in a small town. The project in that sense was very much about flexibility, and we won it because our scheme maintained elasticity both in the approach and in the final building. The brief asked for co-locating a science centre and a university. After we had won, a foundation donated a sum of money and asked us if we could incorporate a concert hall, as they wanted to integrate this into the scheme. Thanks to our flexible approach, this was very easy to do.

MC *So, once again there is the idea of connections and interactions. I do feel, however, that there is a formality to this project, even though a certain openness is also apparent. When did all this happen?*

KHN This was in 2002, and it has just been completed. I think it is a key project, because it addresses new ways of teaching. To achieve the most from the co-location of the private research and the public education, we were very much aware of how to ensure the highest possible level of interaction and synergy between the two. It was before the Ørestad College, but I still think that the ideas of physical and social transparency as well as the dedicated choreography of the life in the buildings represent our approach on education.

✳ Alsion

The brief for the Alsion complex was to create synergy between education, research and commercial activities, bringing together Danish University South and a private Science Park. The aim of the project is to encourage frequent collaboration and knowledge-sharing between the public educational sector and the private research sector for bilateral benefit. At a later stage, the Sønderborg Symphonic Orchestra's Concert Hall was included in the brief.

The relative size and scale of Sønderborg is small, and the new building complex large. This called for a delicate work in terms of the complex's appearance, and led to the concept of a series of buildings with short gable ends that alternate with atria buildings. This concept provides transparency and daylight, and corresponds in scale with the neighbouring harbour typology.

Most offices, laboratories and other work places have an unobstructed view towards the water. The architectural concept made it possible to follow the bending coastline, and adhere to the change of level on the site parallel to the coastline: the tube-like buildings protrude above a parterre floor, mainly fitted with common facilities like the library, canteen and students' club, and also opens to the public passing along the promenade.

The wish for synergy and knowledge-sharing inspired the choreography of life in the building complex. All common facilities are situated in the parterre,

making it necessary for all, students as well as scientists, to 'step down' and meet, exchange knowledge and become personally acquainted — in the restaurant, the library, the club, etc..

The atria buildings were not in the brief — they were made simply by moving the glass wall forward so a traditional comb-structure was enriched with these new tall and light spaces.

When the Concert Hall was later introduced, the serial concept was perfect for adapting yet another element. The railway station challenged the idea of a perfect Concert Hall for symphonic music. However, excellent work by Arup Acoustics, together with the box-in-box concept that fitted 3XN's overall concept, made it possible to listen without disturbance to a single violin. The Danish-Icelandic artist Olafur Eliasson's art is installed on the walls of the Concert Hall foyer. This consists of triangular, titanium glazed tiles, which grow in size upwards, following a mathematical progression.

Outside working hours, the building complex is open to the surrounding community, offering a wide variety of cultural events, using the Concert Hall, auditoria, libraries, meeting rooms, etc.. The entire ground floor is therefore open to everyone at almost anytime. Security is established as a horizontal division from the parterre floor and up — ascent to higher levels requires key cards. Alsion was awarded the RIBA European Award 2007.

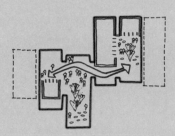

Common functions, ground floor.

Corresponding scale.

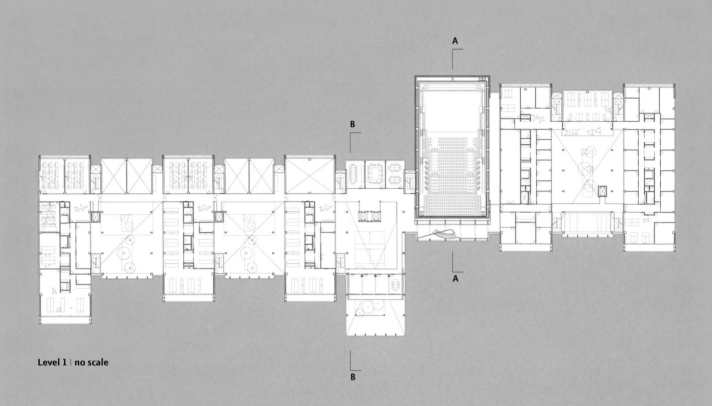

Level 1 | no scale

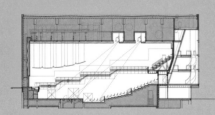

Section AA, concert hall | no scale

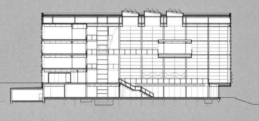

Section BB, main auditorium | no scale

The landscape design plays an important part in the overall perception of the scheme. By using soft and curved lines for the landscaping as opposed to the buildings' regular forms, a positive tension is built up.

The sequences of different levels, from the parterre floor to water surface, establishes a gentle transformation that also has proven useful to both users of the building and other people within the community.

At nightfall the light inside
the glass atria makes the
buildings transparent.

The main atria with
restaurant and an elevated
'meeting box'.

The indoor climate was a focal point. Natural ventilation is driven by the tall atria, and exposed concrete surfaces double as heat storage and regulators. Inside the atria, eight to nine metre tall trees have been installed in order to ensure a healthy atmosphere; visually, as well as physically.

When we work with an artist, we prefer to establish a serious and mutual relationship that is about the art as well as the architecture, and wish for the two to seamlessly become one, instead of the art becoming an adapted decoration.

MC *So, how did it work with Olafur Eliasson? Was it just by chance he came aboard?*

KHN No, we chose him, and as in the Savings Bank, the client followed our recommendations. When we work with an artist, we prefer to establish a serious and mutual relationship that is about the art as well as the architecture, and wish for the two to seamlessly become one, instead of the art becoming an adapted decoration. In public buildings we always work with artists, due to certain rules that we have to follow. In the Alsion project, one of the clients was a foundation who allotted more than the required one per cent for art, so we explored many more possibilities together with Olafur.

MC *So, what was it in your approach that set you apart from the other Danish architects involved in the competition?*

KHN Several things, I guess. We made a very compact building concept, and we respected the scale of the city. We divided the complex into several buildings, but grouped and connected them directly. We had a common ground floor that mixed students and scientists and made them meet each other to exchange ideas. Most of the other proposals worked with large single units, and maybe had different ideas of how to enhance the advantages of co-location. We also engaged closely with the community, so that the University, the Science Centre and the Concert Hall became a group of cultural building that the entire community could use. The resulting shape is not dynamic, but here great attention was paid to the detail of the building volumes.

Concert Hall foyer with art-wall by Olafur Eliasson.

Concert Hall interior.

View from the foyer to the water.

enjoy working

'Barcode' silk screen prints
on Kronjylland facades,
designed by 3XN.

Kronjylland interior with
'pinball traces' in ash wood.

MC *All this contributes to making a successful building, and Olafur's contribution for the foyer walls is stunning I think. Working with artists is very important to you but something special happened in the Kronjylland Savings Bank. Can you tell me about this?*

KHN The initial idea in the Kronjylland project was to ask an artist to work on the facade, but funnily enough, the client thought we could take on the role of artists. So we did, and actually, I think the result was fine. However, what you are probably referring to, is what we exhibited at the 2004 Biennale in Venice; an installation called Listen to the Light, which was the work of the artists Nicoline Refsing and Erik Hougaard Sørensen. They used the facades as enormous screens for their alternating projections, while 300 choral singers and a symphony orchestra performed inside the building, which was transmitted to the public outside via loudspeaker clusters.

MC *When the client said you could take on this role as artists what did he mean by that? Was it in regard to the appearance of the facade?*

KHN It was a reference to the graphics on the glass facade. If you look closely, there are 12 different panels. We silk screen-printed these images and carried out a number of tests before arriving at the final result.

MC *Looking at the project, even though it is obviously transparent and light, it still feels as if it is enclosing something. Can you tell me more about this?*

KHN The concept was very much about creating an inspiring and satisfying working space. Despite the name Kronjylland Savings Bank, the building has no counters and doesn't serve any customers — it's the administration's head offices. The building's first storey with lobby, canteen and reception, is transparent to give staff and visitors a clear view over the surrounding landscape and the river, while the office and meeting room floors above are clad in slate. Circulation is through the inner atrium, which links the ground floor to the office floors and is covered by a glass roof. The internal glass partitions avoid the rigidity of conventional offices. They are movable and interchangeable so that they are able to form different spaces, maintaining a dialogue with the external facade.

MC *I guess this is the sort of flexibility we shall see in the Ørestad College. But if we continue with this argument of an opposing dialogue between the interior and the exterior, the Deloitte project in Copenhagen immediately comes to mind.*

KHN It certainly does, it is very much about the concept of opposing forces, since we tried to render the exterior solidity, with a quality of openness to the interiors.

MC *It does look very compact from the outside — it*

has something of a mechanical fortress about it. But it fascinates me, this play between the interior and exterior in the Deloitte project...

KHN The project was about a dispersed organisation that was going to become one unit, a team. While the outside is closed, or at least quite straightforward and 'clean', the interior is open and vivid. This encourages interaction with long views across the space, while still maintaining a sense of security.

For the climatic protection we worked with a concept of a double skin — two sheets of glass with a wood lamella sandwiched between them. In this case the concept became the building itself, looking at it from the outside. The materials did the talking. In the interior, both we and the client wanted to create a learning organisation. The main staircase inside the large atrium played a significant part in this strategy; so obviously, this was also where the focus of the artist was directed. Here, we worked with the artist Steven Scott, whose art piece works as an essential part of the central atrium.

Deloitte Headquarters, Copenhagen — the central atrium.

✱ Kronjylland Savings Bank

The headquarters of the Kronjylland Savings Bank is situated on the banks of the largest river in Denmark; the Gudenå River, by the town of Randers. The head office — a sharp, monolithic object in a green meadow down to the river's edge — has become a distinctive landmark in Randers' urban picture. Setting ambitious architectural standards, the Kronjylland Headquarters is the first building to be erected on the large site, which is earmarked as a landscaped park comprising solitary buildings.

The building is made up of three elements: a plinth, a glass crystal and a wooden box. The plinth — faced with dark, natural stone — defines a clearly delimited area. The ground floor is surrounded, almost invisibly, by a transparent, recessed facade that creates the illusion that the three-storey 'glass crystal' is floating above the dark plinth. The ground floor includes functions like reception, guest facilities and canteen.

The three floors of the glass crystal are occupied by offices, all positioned against the external facade. The interior of the crystal comprises a high atrium reaching upwards through all three floors, illuminated through a large glass roof. A vertical slice contains all necessary auxiliary rooms. Facing the atrium, a creation in ash wood is tracing the 'trail' of a bouncing ball, zig-zagging between the bottom floor and the glass ceiling.

The outer layer of the facade is coated with a shimmering of crisp, serigraphed glass plates, bearing stripes of varying widths and spacing. In front of the windows they serve as a transparent solar screen but — light and weather permitting — they can swivel to the horizontal to provide a completely unobstructed view.

The final element in the building is a 'box' lined with wood and housing three small guestrooms. The wooden box is wedged between the glass crystal and the plinth near the entrance area, projecting some eight metres out and floating above the ground.

Listen to the light,
August 22, 2004

**77, an art piece by Steven
Scott, dominates the central
atrium. Light fields slowly
change colours under all
bridges and stairways.**

✳ Deloitte Headquarters

The Deloitte Headquarters is not only the
largest of the group of three structures
controlled by a common masterplan,
but is also Denmark's biggest open
office building. Well-connected by public
transportation to the nearby Copenhagen
city centre and Ørestad, it neighbours the
Stadsgraven water reservoir. The buildings
present themselves as solitary volumes on
an edge between land and water.

Green hanging gardens are cut into
the building volume. They create oases
for small breaks and open up to the
daylight. The openings prolong the
facade line, enabling all office areas to
be placed along the outer perimeter,

ensuring optimum panoramic views
and fresh air. The facades are made of
double glass elements. This makes way
for natural ventilation and a protected
place for sunshade blinds.

The office areas and the central
atrium compose one large room. The
result is a transparent organisation with
a high degree of informal knowledge
sharing. The atrium frames one large
piece of art; 77, made of light by Steven
Scott. The stairs and bridges crossing
the atrium display at their bottom
sides fields of lights with varying
widths, changing colours in a cycle that
avoids repetition for several years.

The suggestion here is that one exact
combination of light will not happen
again within a lifetime...

The office areas are largely created as
open landscapes, but numerous back-up
rooms such as study cells and meeting
rooms are at all levels, allowing for
withdrawal and silent contemplation.

Besides the office space, the building
also contains a fitness room, a basement
bar lounge and a circular roof terrace,
cut into the penthouse floor. Below
ground there are two levels of parking,
the lower being an automatic parking
device with lifts.

harlequin

**Informal bar and lounge
in the new Tivoli Pavilion
(above); veiled with
twisted white ribbons that
are transparent from the
inside and create a joyful
'tivolish' pattern on the
outside (opposite).**

MC *Your Tivoli project further explores the evolution
of detail. I think this is a key work for many reasons.
Here, the facade has the appearance of a twisted ribbon.
Where did this idea come from?*

KHN Well, Tivoli, is a funfair, one of the oldest in the
world. It is very much about serpentine waves, and our
design also makes references to the Harlequin character
in his motley patchwork of red, green, and blue
diamonds, because the traditional 'Commedia dell'Arte'
still plays a part in the Tivoli atmosphere. This was a
competition, and the brief was a renovation and an
extension to the existing concert hall and rehearsal
rooms.

MC *What is the leading concept here?*

KHN Well, it is mainly about moving people around.
People come out during the intermission and they need
to find their way around. The solution we adopted was
a circular plinth that unfolds through a central stair.

MC *If we bring up again the argument of the detail as a
study of the facade, in Tivoli you begin to explore the
three-dimensional possibilities of the facade. In the
projects that we have talked about so far, the facades
were two-dimensional. They exploited the quality of the
material, its texture and transparency. Do you think the
Tivoli facade marks a turning point in your work?*

KHN You're right. The Tivoli Pavilion was designed in
2005 after the Ørestad College. A parallel can be drawn
with that scheme; only in Tivoli we used the camera
shutter motif en miniature. However, you can read
in it similarities of the dynamic concepts and vertical
flows, and that is why I consider it to be part of the new
beginning at 3XN.

MC *It's something that you can also read in projects
like the Saxo Bank, where you incorporated a flowing
element in the facade, even though it remains quite
geometrical.*

KHN Well, in the Saxo Bank the facade was even more
important because it was constructed as a fluid shape
— it was not an applied form. Another important
factor was the introduction of new legislation in
Denmark regarding the energy efficiency of buildings.
The amount of glazing in the facade was critical, in
the sense that we were obliged to maintain a balance
between lighting levels internally and meeting the
required environmental standards for maximum heat
loss through the facades.

✳ Tivoli Concert Hall Pavilion

The prestigious task of renovating and extending the Concert Hall in the Tivoli Gardens, Copenhagen's long-famous amusement park was a result of a restricted competition in 2004.

The venerable hall was renovated in keeping with its historical surroundings; the building has been gently improved in order to meet the modern requirements of a Concert Hall. The scene, the orchestra pit, the acoustics, and the comfortable seating should be improved while maintaining the spirit and identity of Tivoli.

A new extension to the Concert Hall is realised in a light, transparent design that matches Tivoli's playful ambience. Twisted aluminium strips with white lacquer provide the right "harlequin" pattern, with a modern, yet playful, look and feel. The new Pavilion houses the new main entrance to the Concert Hall and lounge area, incorporating a bar and a cafe with outdoor service.

A former slot machine hall in the basement under the Concert Hall has been radically transformed into a new lobby with rest rooms and access ways to the Concert Hall and has — as its most spectacular feature — a 30 metre long aquarium covering one of the lobby walls. The aquarium is the main light provider to the lobby.

The brief also included the construction of a new large rehearsal hall for the Tivoli Symphony Orchestra as well as for visiting orchestras. The building is situated on the Tivoli perimeter facing Tietgen's Street, and includes improved staff facilities, a Wagamama restaurant on ground floor level and a conference centre set on top of the rehearsal hall with a view to the Tivoli gardens.

three-dimensionality

MC *Looking into the future, I can see the Liverpool project taking the three-dimensional thinking in the facade one step further. You were telling me that the detailing was essential and that it should have a dialogue with the details of the existing surrounding buildings.*

KHN That's right. Here it was a question of playing with a kind of dynamic relief that would maintain and enhance the whole concept of flows. At the same time, it needed to have a certain amount of detail so as to be able to interact with the Three Graces. In the end, we came up with a three-dimensional pattern that really evolved with the project.

MC *And from that, you moved to an even more a fluid facade, where the detailing and three-dimensionality plays with the site itself. I am referring to the Lighthouse project that we discussed previously.*

KHN Well, in the Lighthouse project we developed this further; the detailing made the facade a three-dimensional object, and this is what gives character to

the buildings. This strategy helps placing the building complex into the context; it gives a greater meaning to the facade; a sculptural reference to the reflections of light in the waves.

MC *But I guess that you really pushed the boundaries with the Am Kaffeelager project. Here, you clearly experience that the facade has become the building. Can you tell me how this project came about?*

KHN It was for a competition — which we didn't win. The project was in the Harbour City in Hamburg, for a site right by the water. Eric van Egeraat had drawn up the masterplan and he talked about the concept of a canyon between the buildings. Our response was to make a building that would have a certain roughness to it. The idea came about as a sort of origami; paper folding. As we developed the project, we became more and more influenced by the site — by the harbour and the sails. In the end, you can see that the facade had assumed a sail-like structure, and although it appears to have a complex form, it is simple and repetitive.

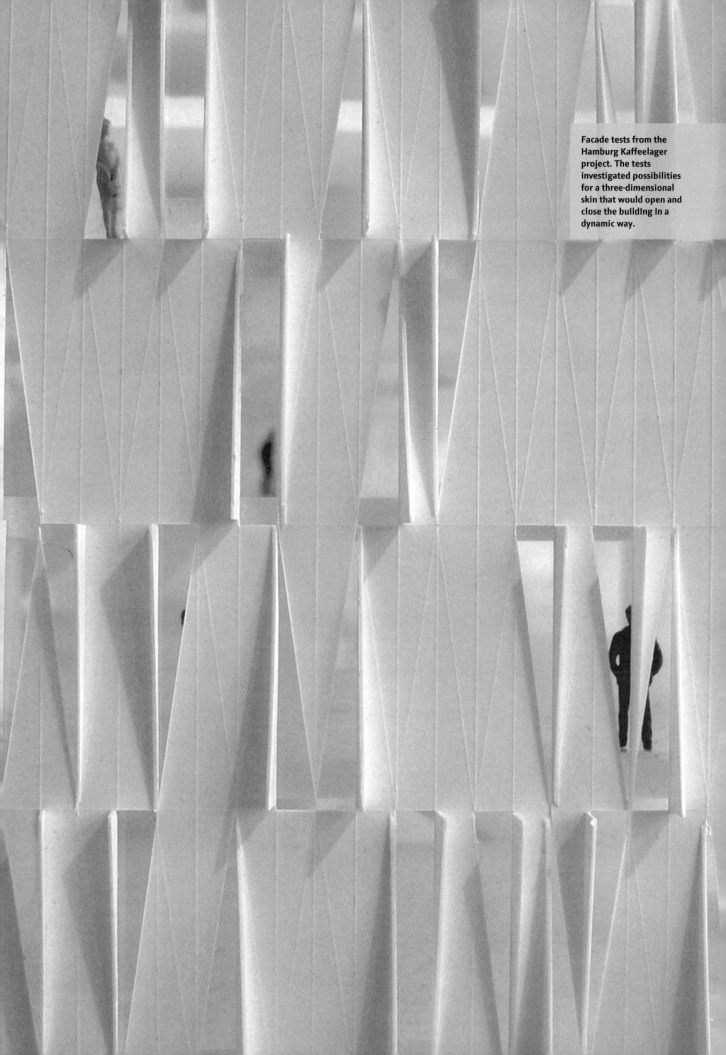

Facade tests from the Hamburg Kaffeelager project. The tests investigated possibilities for a three-dimensional skin that would open and close the bullding In a dynamic way.

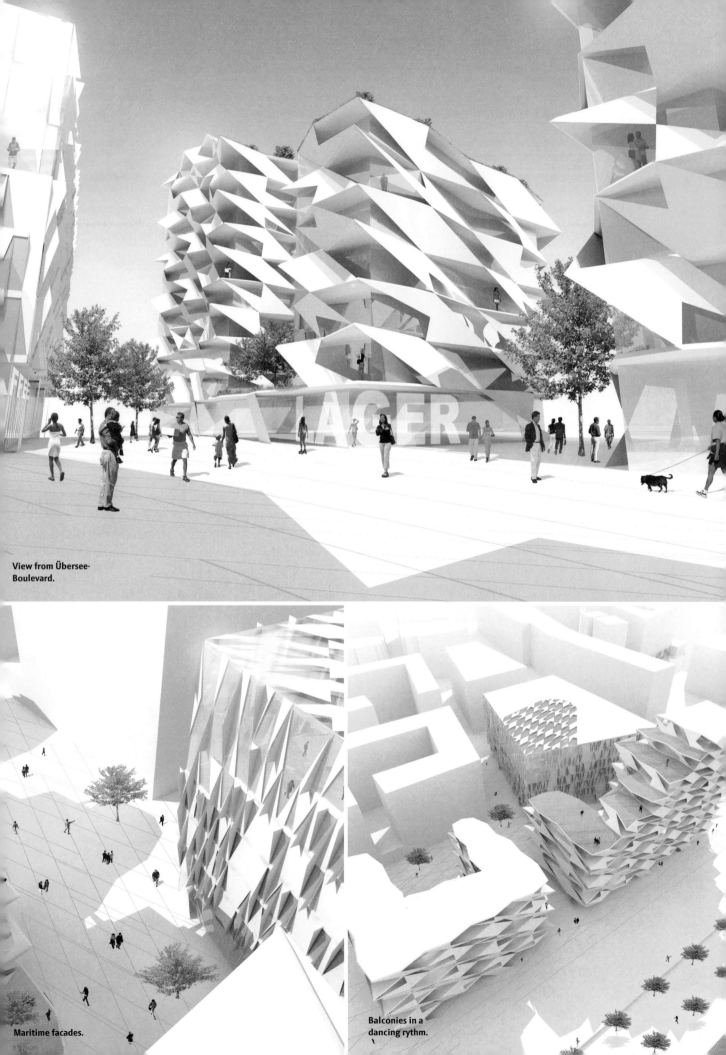

View from Übersee-Boulevard.

Maritime facades.

Balconies in a dancing rythm.

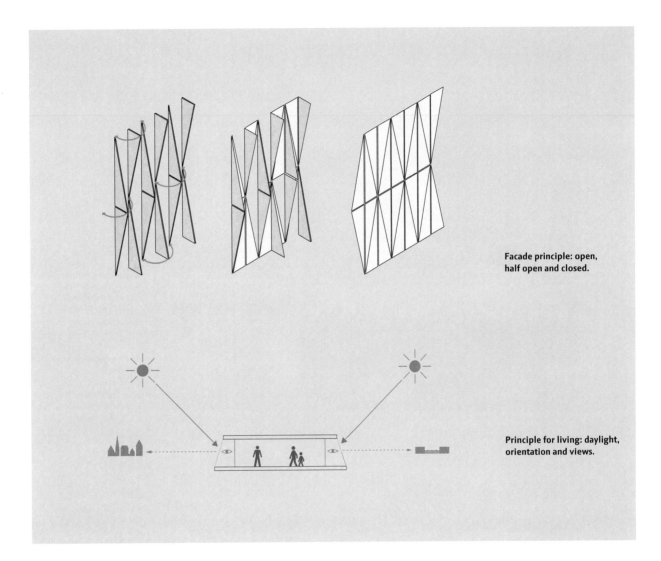

Facade principle: open,
half open and closed.

Principle for living: daylight,
orientation and views.

✳ Am Kaffeelager

The residential and office building project "Am Kaffeelager" was designed in competition for a significant plot in the new maritime city centre, Hamburg Harbour, in Hamburg, Germany. The two residential buildings and the office block mediate between the new and the old parts of the city, and mark the entrance to a long shopping boulevard that connects to the future cruise terminal.

The design adheres to the situation by the sea with its white rhomb-shaped slates. They create a light 'paper collage', staggered in front of large windows, in contrast to the large ships

in the harbour. The vision is to create a three-dimensional expression that plays with light and gives the sort of richness in details lacking in many modern buildings.

The expression is contemporary, and within a reasonable budget. The basic structure of the buildings is rational and straight-forward. The facade is not load-bearing and was therefore chosen as the arena for the architectural expression. Balconies are prefab elements that mount to the floor decks with no thermal bridge. The balconies are not rectangular; they have triangular shapes which allow for wider areas for

sitting outside, combined with more narrow areas, suitable for window cleaning. The shifting of these balconies from floor to floor creates a dancing rhythm and lends a three-dimensionality to the facade.

A light outer shell connects the balconies and doubles as a sun screen. The result is a sculptural facade with dynamic and detailed expression, and with the rhomb-figure as a common marker for all three buildings, only in various shapes: as filigree in the office building, and as movable balcony railing in the residential buildings.

innovative solutions

The building construction business has much to learn. 3XN's R&D department seeks inspiration from other fields about materials, techniques and approaches to strengthen the innovative process within architecture. (America's Cup yacht, top left; Formula One car, bottom left; America's Cup sail manufacturing, right).

MC *So I guess that this is where your new research department comes into play. Having pushed the limits in a three-dimensional sense, you look deeper into materiality and consider the sustainability aspects. I agree with you that, currently, materials are not fully exploited within the discourse on sustainable and energy-efficient architecture. So this research is very important to understand how the inherent qualities of materials can help to push for more efficient and innovative solutions.*

KHN That's exactly it. Our research department had a lot to do with this project. The client didn't quite follow us and we didn't have the resources to fully investigate and consequently explain which materials would be optimum to use. At that point, I thought that it would be a good idea to have a department that would help us to develop our ideas at an early stage. This research is started with sustainability as a point of departure, and it brings us further, and provides us with new answers and new solutions. This doesn't necessarily mean using hyper-technology and expensive materials, but it helps us to understand more deeply and know a range of materials and their potential for creating new and better solutions.

MC *So it is pushing the limits of your architecture, and linking it to other disciplines that have already experimented with materiality and execution.*

KHN That's what we are trying to do here. The research department becomes a useful tool for compctitions. We are often faced with questions on the proposed materials, sustainability and build-ability of our designs, and we don't want to repeat what happened with the Kaffeelager competition.

MC *I think that it is essential to make this a design tool, to further assimilate new technology, not just as an instrument for superficial experimental form. There will be a type of architect who uses information as the substance of a new form of architecture. However, there must be a distinction between the computational design that produces shapes and design that is generated from the data itself.*

KHN Certainly. We want to be at ease with the digital age in which we live. Everything seems to be changing quickly, especially in architecture, but the building industry still responds slowly. As a result, we are looking at the developments in other fields and disciplines, from medicine to space technology to Formula One cars. It's all about creating a link, because new technology gives you a creative freedom, resulting in work that is optimised and refined.

Our work can be divided into two areas, digital technology and developments in the world of materials. With these, you can have a completely new approach, ecologically and even structurally.

MC *Well, I agree — the ecological aspects of design have to be brought back into the discourse. By this, I mean not just on an aesthetic design level, but in a more meaningful way.*

KHN That's why we have been doing this research. One of the outcomes is that our department has produced articles for the Danish press, commenting on new technologies and how these developments from different fields can be used in architecture, to improve energy consumption, etc.. We've looked at new textiles, composites, nanotechnology, direct manufacturing, and space materials like aero-gel for translucent insulation. Subsequently, we've looked into the materials used in the construction of yachts similar to those developed for the America's Cup. We visited Nevada to see how they manufacture sails the size of soccer fields. We realised that this was a beautiful example of how the use of digital technologies and designed materials can lead to quick production and optimised form and function.

Self-cleaning lotus leaf; bullet-proof aramid fibres; lightweight stiff carbon fibres; phase-changing polymer pockets; acoustical non-woven textile; insulating translucent aerogel (top left to bottom right).

material architecture

Scientists can achieve a
very high level of control
in modern material
architecture. An example is
the large-scale innovation
going on within non-woven
textiles, as variously
illustrated here.

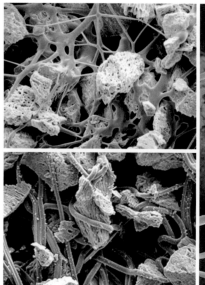

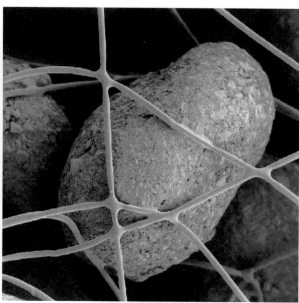

By incorporating active
carbon, textiles become
self-cleaning — thermally
glued, top left; chemically
bonded, bottom left;
mechanically trapped, right.

Electrospinning; an
electrical charge forms a
mat of fine fibres.

Lamp design. 3XN's R&D department tests the work flow from digital design (left) through 3-D printing to physical prototype (above).

MC *So, I guess that the true challenge is the link between the digital world and the physical world, how other technologies are at the forefront of material use, offering new possibilities?*

KHN I agree, because in the digital world everything is possible, and as you said earlier, it needs to be applied back to reality. And that's what we are experimenting with. Dreams of digital architecture are fascinating but not if we can't realise our dreams. Initially, we started testing the new furniture for our office using laser cutting and CNC milling, and then with the design of lamps in rapid prototyping.

MC *Another field that has always fascinated me, in that sense, is the movie industry. I think it provides an eye-opener with many possibilities.*

KHN That's true — it's amazing what can be achieved on movie sets. The movie industry is a good example of how advances in other industries can be highly relevant to our field. What has been achieved with digital manipulation opens a whole new box of design tools. Imagine this interview a few years ago, words like 'animated' and 'algorithmic design' wouldn't have existed. Another thing we can learn from the movie industry is how well they communicate with people. I believe architectural communication will change radically within a few years; going from flat drawings to three-dimensional and alive experiences.

MC *The other thing that we were talking about was the use of different materials. There are quite a number of material libraries popping up in Europe. Is that what you are looking to do?*

KHN No, we will just use the existing ones and pick the relevant materials from them. It's a question of closing that gap between technology and architecture.

If you use nanotechnology, the basic structure and composition of materials can be manipulated, which means that our design phase already starts at the material level. Materials can become heat accumulating or self-cleaning. The technology of textiles has come a long way. The new frontier is non-woven materials, which give great flexibility.

MC *I think this is fascinating, because if you really look at the range of materials out there, the possibilities are endless.*

KHN I agree, but I think that our R&D department is still at the beginning, and it is going to take time to be able to incorporate this process, and make our teams aware of these technologies and their potential. Architecture should reflect society and the time we are living in, and that is what we are trying to do.

MC *I believe that, at a certain point, you will start the process by designing the material itself. This brings us back to understanding the early use of the detail. As we have already mentioned, in the Music Building it is the materials that give the building its atmosphere, and it was the selection of those materials that made it such a success.*

KHN The Music Building truly benefits from its maritime, quite raw materiality. Detailing and the choice of materiality represent the final transformation from design to reality. In taking the project from beginning to end. With this technology, you can reach a whole new level of design. In the future, every time one uses a material it should be with a highly dedicated purpose, as with medicine for a particular illness. Our hope is that our research will provide the opportunities to pick the best material for each project.

build

communities

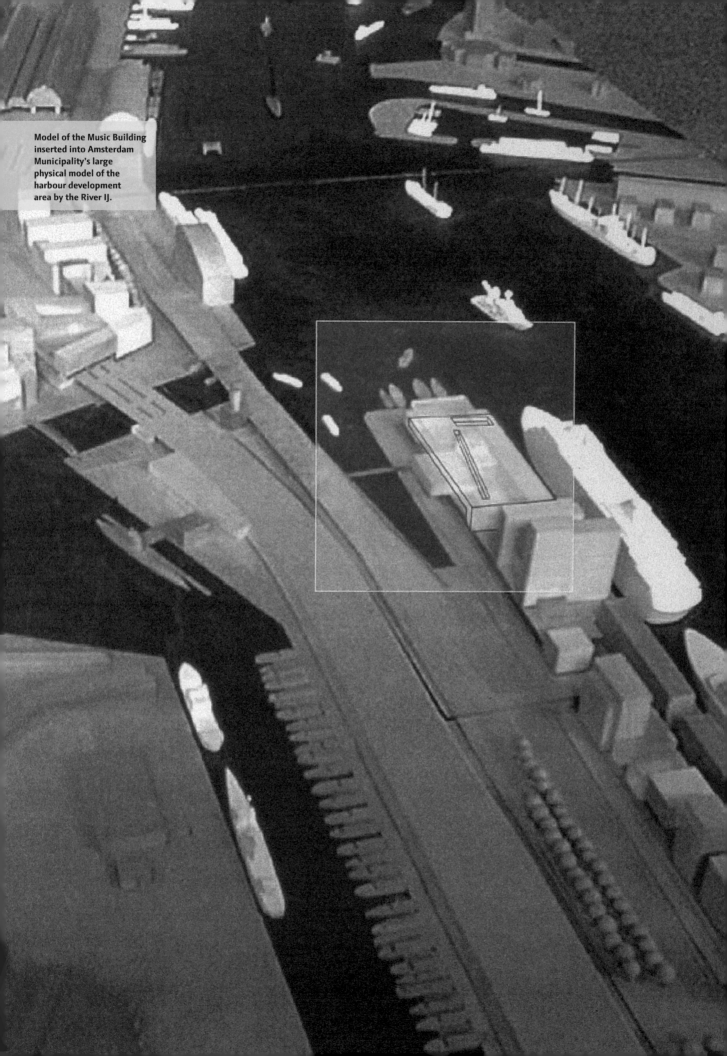

Model of the Music Building inserted into Amsterdam Municipality's large physical model of the harbour development area by the River IJ.

building a community

Oosterlijke Handelskade used to be part of Amsterdam's industrial harbour. 3-D illustrations from the municipality masterplan showing the future full development scheme with the Music Building as 'attractor' at the pier head.

MC *The Music Building was not only about the detailing and the bringing of the project from concept to build, but also to do with the site and the community. The most prominent effect of this project was the positive stimulation it had on the area; the Music Building has become a gathering space for the community, not just a cultural entity?*

KHN The resonance that the Music Building has had is impressive. As I said before, the choice of materials and detailing contributes to the warm and informal atmosphere that many have emphasised.

But you're right; mainly, it has been about building a community — in two ways: firstly, the effect of the building was expanding the existing city core to embrace the former trading pier and in this way expand focus and make this place culturally more important in Amsterdam, whilst secondly bringing together two rather different musical communities; the IJsbreker and the BIMHuis.

The project was inaugurated in 2005, but the competition actually took place ten years ago, and we had to come up with the scheme in only two weeks at the time. The brief required that we housed two different musical institutions in one building, letting each maintain their own identity, yet still creating this landmark. What came out was the concept of two volumes playing and reacting to each other.

The sense of community is not static. The integration of harbour areas has extended the urban city core and this has diminished 'mental distances'. The Music Building is just a five minute walk from the Central Station.

✱ Muziekgebouw

The Music Building brings together two well-established cultural institutions; the Muziekgebouw (former known as the Ijsbreker) and the BIMhuis jazz club, at a new common location; the spectacular head of the Piet Heinkade. The building fulfils the masterplan ambition to create an attractor for public life at this newly developed site in Amsterdam, and a landmark facing the fjord IJ, yet dissolves into details in human scale on approach.

The high degree of exposure played a significant role in the development of the architectural concept. The building has five almost equally important facades: two towards the fjord; one towards the city and the water basin Zouthaven; one towards the neighbouring hotel and suspended plaza, and last but not least the roof; the fifth facade which is highly visible from the adjacent hotel and the enormous

cruise ships that harbour at the pier from time to time.

The internal structure also influenced the design. In order to achieve a truly public building, a 24 hour 'open flow' was designed, regardless of the activities in the BIMhuis or the Muziekgebouw. The building is the culmination of a long public promenade, which is elevated by two floors in order to create visual contact with downtown Amsterdam. Via wide staircases, the promenade connects to the pier level and the water, and becomes the spectacular access route to the interior. Thus it has been possible to keep a democratic ideal and appeal to a broad public.

Transparency is one of the most important aspects of the building. The large glazed front reveals the interior to the surroundings with the opportunity

to experience it from different levels, on different platforms, at diverse angles, and in an ever-changing way. Though the overall layout gestures towards the IJ, the building still addresses all directions; interacting with the different light -, water -, weather conditions, and the time of day.

The play of light, both daylight and electric light, are consciously used to influence the appearance of the building: regarding the impact of the sun, with large glass facades letting in a flood of daylight; filtered, softened and protected by the cantilevered roof. Once inside, the daylight shapes the different building elements, while LED light features inside the Muziekgebouw concert hall are able to pulsate according to the rhythm of the music, or simply support the musical atmosphere by changing light and colour.

There is little difference
between the first concept
model (this page) and
the model of the finished
building (opposite) but
thorough investigations
and six years lie between.

the 'cap'

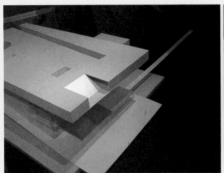

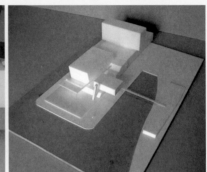

A point of investigation was the 'cap'. The first vision was a one-storey element with offices and outdoor amphi-theatre. It was tried without this element, but finally it was decided that a thin cap should be included in the scheme.

MC *You perceive this unity from a distance and upon entering you can see how the concept dissolves into several entities, with the central stair as a connector. I think that the project developed with the void becoming a space in itself. One can clearly see this from the early stages, and how it developed and evolved through time.*
KHN Initially, after we won the competition, we started building various models and came up with a very simple diagram: we had a plinth that contained all the technical and rehearsal facilities to prepare the music; a public area with concert halls to perform the music, and a top cap to preserve the music, with library, documentation centre, etc....
MC *You even had outdoor spaces.*
KHN Interaction with the site was the main idea, and part of the city of Amsterdam's request was to create a public space. This was imperative as every year Amsterdam holds a music festival with various events scattered throughout the city. So, the stairs became a kind of outdoor theatre since performances often took place outside.

In our initial plans we had an outdoor concert hall built into the 'cap' floor. Unfortunately there was no budget for the library and documentation centre, which affected the total budget so we could not afford the cap. We had to rethink the concept, so we took the top 'cap' floor out of the project. This had a very big impact on the building and stopped progress on the project for a year. Without the 'cap', the elements seemed lost at sea, so to speak. They needed this connecting element.
MC *But fortunately in the end it was restored, because it really looks bare without it.*
KHN It did, also because after all, the client had known it for so long and had got used to it, so even to them the building looked like something was missing without the 'cap'. However, it was a process that went really slowly. This is best illustrated by the fact that during this long period we started using computers and integrating them in our office.

First concept model. The 'cap' contains all office and exhibition space. This was later moved to the back of the building but the roof was needed visually to embrace the different elements, especially to establish the sought-for landmark identity when observed from a distance.

The informal character encourages many sorts of activities. The Music Building has had a major positive impact on Amsterdam, even Dutch, community life.

The two music institutions needed their own individual identity. Foyer decks outside the large concert hall of Muziekgebouw (this page) and stairway to the BIMhuis jazz club (opposite).

Restaurant in
front at pier level.

Entrance to the
Muziekgebouw
Concert Hall.

'Canyon-like' stepped access between the Muziekgebouw Concert Hall and BIMhuis.

Integration. Three foyer decks suspended into the public space.

View from the outdoor
plinth to River IJ and
Central Station.

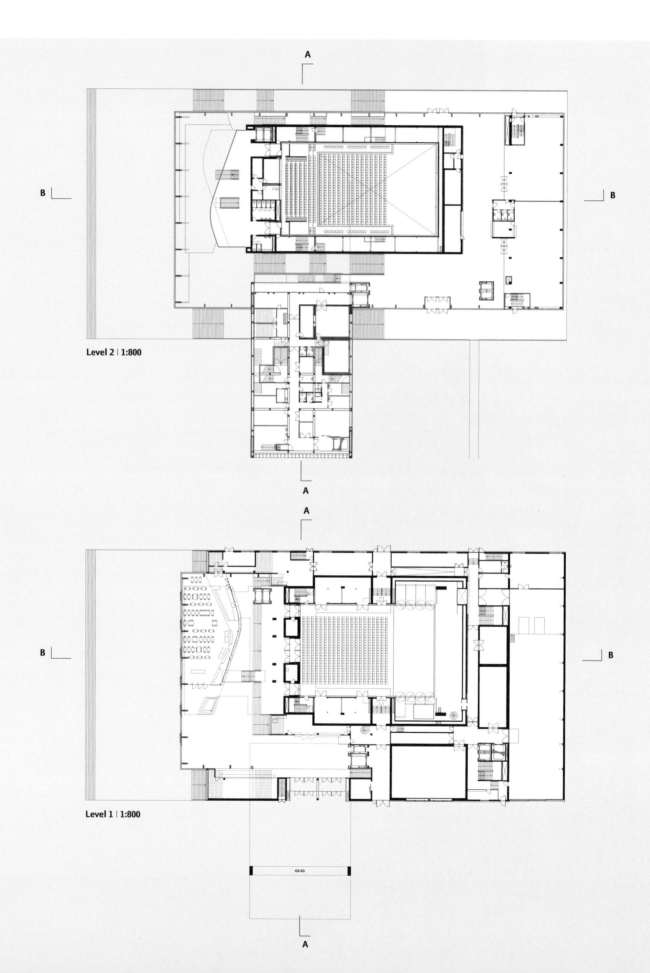

Level 2 | 1:800

Level 1 | 1:800

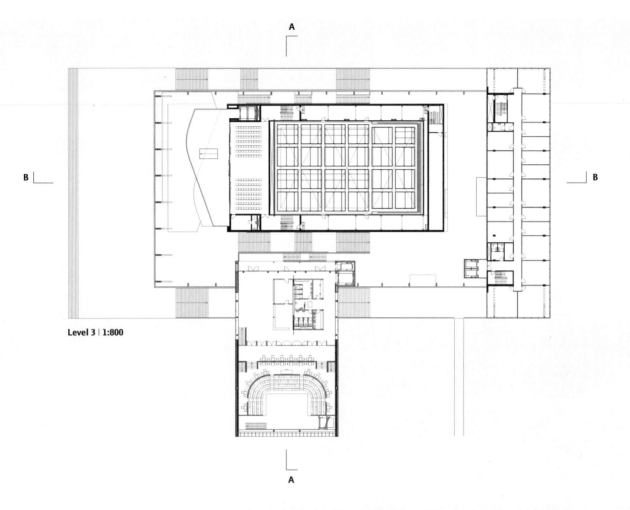

Level 3 | 1:800

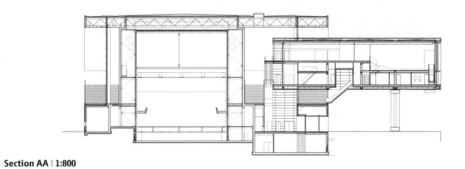

Section AA | 1:800

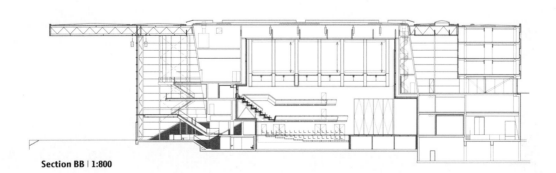

Section BB | 1:800

The large concert hall is used for a wide range of purposes, not only for music. Gala dinner and conference.

concert hall

The story there was that we had to provide new common premises for two well-established institutions, the Ijsbreker and the BIMhuis.

MC *Can you tell me more about the IJsbreker's large concert hall and its flexible space?*

KHN We wanted to do something that was more specific than just a black box. With our solution, with the wooden walls mounted with LEDs, not only did we solve various problems that had arisen, but we also gave the space an identity. We chose to cooperate with the artist Steven Scott, who came up with the original ideas for creating this unique atmosphere of light inside the large concert hall.

We also designed the restaurant and all the furniture to keep the design as one entity and to care for our concept. The expenses turned out to be extremely modest for a building of its kind, partly because of our well-considered use of materials. I think you can say that we made budget constraints a virtue, and went for a robust expression, that actually goes very well with the notion of a 'public living room' that was one of the aims. People feel welcome, and that is definitely part of the project's success.

The large concert hall is
equipped with hidden LEDs
to create glowing colourful
walls; variable over time
in different fields and even
along with the music (these
and following pages).

Arrival and applause.

jazz at BIMhuis

MC *The two entities had to get used to being under one roof, didn't they?*

KHN If I think back, the BIMhuis was reluctant to move in together with the IJsbreker; after all they did not share the same audience, with the IJsbreker catering for modern improvisational music and the BIM being this world famous smoky jazz club, and in fact they were also quite satisfied with their existing club, though they needed more space. So in order to make the jazz people feel at home, we simply copied their original layout and placed it exactly the same way in the project. On top of that, we made a big window so they could look back to where they were situated before and also enjoy a view of the city lights, which I believe is in the spirit of jazz. Funnily enough, they were not happy with it. They didn't believe that a jazz club could do with a window — but in the end they were convinced and it was a huge success! At the opening concert, the curtain was closed, but when the concert started it slid back and opened for the stunning view of Amsterdam's night lights to become the perfect backdrop for the scene, and the whole crowd cheered. The truth is that good architecture gives people what they didn't know that they wanted! Today, the BIMhuis has more than doubled the number of visitors, and they have been able to develop a professional organisation; coming from using staff subsidised by the state. Living together with IJsbreker, or the Muziekgebouw as they call themselves nowadays, also seems to work out quite well. I think they experience a sort of synergy effect that is similar to the one in the Alsion Research and University project in Denmark that we discussed previously.

The large bay window in the BIMhuis makes an urban backdrop with a view to Amsterdam.

ZAAL LINKS >>

MC *Didn't you win several awards for the Music Building?*

KHN Yes we did — and I have a funny story about one of them, The Nederlandse Bouwprijs (the Dutch Building Award). I was late for the ceremony, arriving just in time for the announcement of the 'Building of the Year' award. Upon entering I went straight up to the stage, but the client got there seconds before me to collect the award — he still has it, even as we speak! This story goes to tell that when the result is positive, the client is ready to take credit, whereas if someone needs to be blamed for something going wrong it's usually the architect! However, I prefer a happy client, who loves the final result so much that he is ready to believe he practically designed the building by himself; that's when we have done a fine job...!

MC *Exactly. As we were saying, the project has been a huge success at a community level. Does that only originate from your design, or are there other factors involved as well?*

KHN It's a combination. If you think about it, this project has lots of qualities that derive from our dispositions — apart from the actual design in our office, Many things have contributed to the uniqueness that is part of the reason for the Amsterdammers' embracing of the building, and it also lies in the planning before we entered the scene. Our efforts to give the harbour and institutions an identity whilst simultaneously revitalising the site and creating a landmark were all in line with the area's original masterplan, designed by OMA. They appointed each new harbour development area with a so-called anchor point; an attractor of life and a carrier of this particular area's identity. For this pier, the anchor point was foreseen to be the Music Building.

urban landscape

MC *It certainly has fulfilled the concept of building a community; I think it is also the strength of a design that helps regenerate an area. One project that really focused on this aspect was the Rainbow project?*

KHN That's right; in the Rainbow project, a sensible coherence with the surrounding community, which is always essential in an urban project, was supplied with the need for creating a strong internal community feel inside the project, mainly because of the magnitude of it. Our first step in approaching a project is literally cutting out the entire brief as little foam blocks and placing them on a site plan, followed by the investigations of the site and the site morphologies. In the Rainbow project, the plot ratio (built area in relation to site area) was 750 so it was all a question of being able to play with the actual programme whilst still being respectful towards the site and creating meaningful relations inside the complex as well as with the surrounding city. The latter was further being complicated by the fact that one of the streets lining the site consisted of listed, low scale (and extremely expensive) houses. In the Rainbow project, the resulting solution, after investigating the site, had quite a different approach than the Liverpool project. I think one needs to design what one finds to be the best solution for given circumstances — the most appropriate, fitting and, eventually, the most beautiful. We were asked to come up with a high quality, high density residential and mixed-use development. And what was also key to the Rainbow project was that it had to be approved by the local residents.

MC *So, this time the research on the site was not only topographical and morphological, but about the cityscape, and how the surrounding inhabitants would be affected by the scheme?*

KHN What we did here, from the beginning, was play with massing models; we took the entire programme and placed it on the site. We then started to play, arriving at possible options. We had to look at the characteristics and understand what the specific needs regarding light, views and heights were.

MC *And you also had to play with aspects of the city's morphology, in that it isn't just about the specific site, but how the building is placed in the context and topography of Dublin.*

KHN Yes. We played with the existing framework, meaning that we responded to Dublin's context, from the classical, low-rise older houses, to the eight- or nine-storey newer hotels and towers in the area. The banal point of departure was the fact that if one were to simply stack the programme onto the site it would be too massive. At this point we started shaping it, trying to make it slim, dynamic and have a sense of openness. The solution turned out to be similar to a rollercoaster, with strong vertical dimensions but at the same time comprising a smooth low-rise profile at the level of the surrounding streets. The major part of the massing was subtracted from the centre of the site, away from the streets. This had a decisive effect on the scale of the complex.

We wanted to build an 'urban landscape' that would play with the characteristics of the site and the surrounding buildings. We also wanted to add an ecological aspect to the scheme, as we had done in the Liverpool project. The resulting shape was a figure of eight, which gave a playful line to the street, gently undulating in its horizontal planes while also offering green open balconies to a great number of the apartments and offices. This also rendered the architecture with a very vigorous appearance.

Rainbow project, Dublin — brief as foam blocks, stacked on the site. A high-density project is always a challenge in getting local approval.

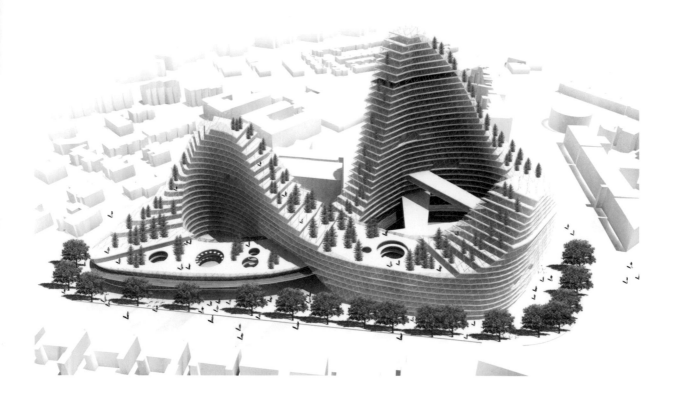

✳ Rainbow project

For a key site in Dublin, Ireland, 3XN was invited to propose a solution for a high-density residential and mixed-use development. The brief comprised residential and serviced apartments; retail, restaurant and bars; offices, fitness and health centres to serve the residents and occupiers of the complex; a boutique 100 bedroom four star hotel; a 300 seat multi-purpose theatre, a multi-purpose exhibition space; two crèches with direct access to a safe protected outdoor play space; a sky lobby for residents with a small cinema, meeting rooms and a private bar lounge with direct access to roof garden or balcony.

Indicative plot ratios were 2.5 to 3 and indicative site coverage was 80 per cent. However, the client expected to achieve a significantly higher plot ratio — a development of 200,000 square metres — through excellence of design.

This building proposal is designed as a 'wave' eddying rhythmically in a figure of eight on the site, as one unbroken building. The building opens above and below into softly rounded passageways inviting people, light and scenic panoramas. Street spaces have a human dimension. The undulating building washes across the site in crested waves, generating landmarks which dynamically peak. Verdant gardens, both as private terraces and larger, common roof gardens, help define the building.

The horizontal figure of eight plan of the building makes it possible to create a slim, dynamic building carcase, with open courtyards. These courtyards form part of the ground floor areas and are covered over by glass structures.

The building's figure of eight design gives it a playful line towards the street. At this level, the building undulates gently in the horizontal plane, offering the street — and the city — small green breathing spaces. Some of these areas would have trees from the old botanical gardens, other areas are new, green pauses in the city. Still, the building continues to give clear definition to the street space.

This way, the proposal includes addressing the sensitivity of the protected neighbouring row of houses, the appropriateness of higher buildings at corners of the site, as well as the retention of mature trees. The layout secures the opening of a large portion of the site to public access, mindful, though, of the quality and exclusivity required for the residential units.

3XN passed on to Stage 2, the client was enthusiastic, but decided to go for a less challenging proposal in order to pass authority approval as quickly as possible. 3XN has been engaged by the client to develop similar design strategies for another site in Dublin.

Rainbow project, first stage. The 'rollercoaster' solution brings major parts of the mass to the back of the site; away from the streets.

Stage 1

continuous flow

MC *It is a sensitive adaptation that, I think, neither ignores nor loses Dublin's present qualities. Was this project a competition or a direct commission?*

KHN It was a competition — ten architects' teams were invited and three of us went through to a final stage for the scheme. Anyway, as I was telling you, if you stacked the desired building mass equally on the site it would be quite massive. What we did was to start shaping it till we got a kind of rollercoaster form. Obviously, it couldn't look like Manhattan skyscrapers due to Dublin's profile at large; it had to be more integrating and inviting since it was going to benefit and be used by the entire community. The important thing is that a building has to add to a site, bring a positive addition that will raise its profile. We worked with a lot of 3-D models, and this is another important aspect of the way we work: we always refer back and forth from the foam block model to the 3-D model, with insertions into the context using a combination of computer renderings and on-site photos.

MC *I can see that the project played with flows and this continues on the discourse we had on surfaces, and the Moebious strip. Looking at it as the project developed you seemed to have changed the harmony of it.*

KHN Well, the first scheme we did was much more balanced and evenly distributed. It had some advantages and some disadvantages. We put the residential area on top of the office spaces, and at the bottom we had retail space. It was a mixture of things, but the client in the end wanted all the functions to be separated and that made the scheme weaker.

MC *So what was your concept initially?*

KHN Well, we wanted it to be more of an urban project, you know, more like a landscape. Today there is a big hotel there with a park. Our idea was to continue the park so that the surrounding buildings could use it too. We studied how best to enter the building, where to put the actual commercial areas and how to create activity at ground level. We created a huge courtyard that would be filled with light. Around it we placed shops and cultural institutions, like a library or a museum, so as to recreate a kind of plaza effect. Then the client decided they wanted a sports centre, so we even created a running track. The lightness and transparency of the building was essential to us as well. The building had openings all over it so that natural light could come through — that is, making it more permeable. The weakness of the scheme, however, was that it was one continuous flow, a single scheme and this would be a problem for the phasing of the project.

MC *Well if you want to find a weakness, you can in every project; it's just how you look at it and what you're looking for. You were showing me that in the second scheme everything changed.*

KHN It did because the client wanted an even larger scheme, and that everything was individual separated entities, meaning the residential, the commercial and the cultural structures stood alone as single buildings. They wanted a lot of flexibility and this disrupted the whole scheme and made it more like towers. Thinking back, the first scheme had more quality regarding integration and the possibility to build upon a community than the second scheme allowed for. I agree that it kind of loses the magic. In the end we came in second!

Stage 1

Community-specific considerations such as contextual integration, mass distribution and functional programming are combined with site-specific parameters. The result in Stage 1 was one unbroken building with a radical, yet soft and friendly shape; a 'wave' eddying rhythmically in a never-ending figure of eight on the site. Verdant gardens; private terraces, as well as large common roof gardens, continue existing park facilities to preserve a 'green' expression.

The Rainbow project fits into Dublin's unifying levels.

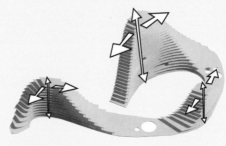

Individual vertical access to dwellings.

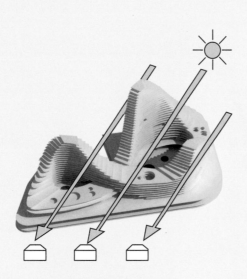

Dividing building mass into slender sections opens for sunlight to pass through.

'Endless' looping office flow in the figure of eight.

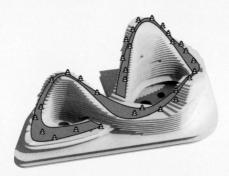

... like dwellings in a green valley....

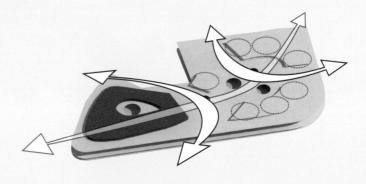

Public pedestrian flows crossing the site.

Stage 1

The undulating building washes across the site in crested waves, generating striking landmarks which dynamically peak — withdrawn to the back of the site, in order to diminish the scale experienced from the street. Dwellings are concentrated in the quieter areas near the centre of the site, away from traffic noise. One building volume containing homes is located centrally in the relative quiet of an adjacent secondary road. This ensures functional diversity here, and echoes the buildings directly across the road, which mainly comprise housing. The road will be busy around the clock. This will have a favourable effect on security and the general feeling of well-being in the area.

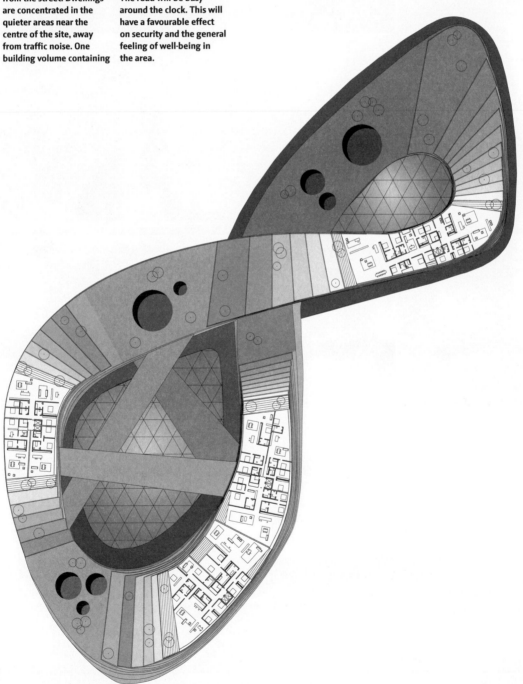

Stage 2

Marie Hesseldahl Larsen, Rasmus Kruse, Jan Amundsen and Kim Herforth Nielsen in a Rainbow working session.

Stage 2

For Stage 2, a revision of the simplicity of the scheme was needed. Mainly because the client could not accept mixing functions in the towers; business areas and dwellings should be kept in separate towers. This had a certain impact on the concept — with more towers, but with many original qualities preserved from Stage 1.

Development of the concept.

... like dwelling in a green valley...

Each residential lobby stretches between two cores and thereby serves twice as many apartments.

The number of office lobbies cab be increased by covering the 'valleys' and creating an atrium space.

The building is divided into a public zone facing the exposed corners while the private zone is facing a quieter area.

Well distributed volumes give free views and no overviewing.

Dividing building mass — opens for sunlight to pass through.

The four office blocks can be occupied by several individual companies or one 35,000 square metre company on the NW corner and a smaller 15,000 square metre company on the NE corner.

North elevation | no scale

South elevation | no scale

Stage 2

Bridges short-cut the retail
courtyards on several levels.

The soft tower model opens the building mass and helps to diminish the street front dominance.

Stage 2

Retail strategies mainly involve street frontage to attract a sufficient amount of customers, and this goes hand in hand with planning aspirations for ensuring activity and life in the urban environment. The inner courtyards were some of the scheme's qualities preserved from Stage 1, and they combine a long street frontage with an urban intimacy that contradicts the high plot ratio and large scale of the project. Working model (these pages) and 3-D renders (overleaf).

Stage 2

Nordhavnen Residences.
Working model, the first
three floor plans.

prefab
morphology

MC *Another project that I wanted to discuss with you which deals with the community is the Nordhavnen Residences. Now this is on a completely different scale to the Rainbow, and in that sense it has a lot to do with an approach to scale. It was talked about a lot, and it also plays with the revitalising of the area.*

KHN Yes, this project won an award in its present form, which we are developing for a client for a site in the Copenhagen North Harbour, hence the name. But the Nordhavnen Residences scheme actually originates from a competition that we didn't win. The masterplan called for an 'amorph' or softly shaped building, but the client at the same time said it had to be buildable and cost-effective. What we came up with was the idea of a very straightforward circular core that had prefab boomerang-shaped mounted terraces; slightly unevenly juxtaposed so as to give everybody light and a view. This was an economical way to obtain a softly shaped and highly unique building. Our current client has not yet been able to acquire a suitable site, but I'm hoping to see this built and prove that a rational budget and high individuality is possible at one and the same time!

**Copenhagen docklands,
the North Harbour.
The residential towers
placed into the existing
context along the
harbour and canals.**

Elliptical balcony elements are 'randomly' attached to circular floor decks.

✱ Nordhavnen Residences

Copenhagen is expanding rapidly on its former docklands, including Nordhavnen — the North Harbour. While most developments have continued traditional urban building strategies or adapted, for instance, Dutch canal houses, this project tries to point to a new direction. It responds to demands established by analysing the modern urban lifestyle without prejudice. Among others, individuality and identity prove to have become major priorities when people select new places to live.

In the Nordhavnen Residences, circular floor plan buildings in a free site plan have replaced traditional urban grid plans, while maintaining, even optimising, density. Circular buildings without corners provide for better views and more daylight for each apartment;

wind turbulence is avoided by the aerodynamic design; and they have an optimum balance between floor area and facade, meaning high spatial and energy efficiency.

The image of a 'pile of plates' is achieved by using balcony additions to each floor — with varied positions. Two balconies are cast onto each floor, turning the rational circular floor plan elliptical in an economical way: the balconies are prefab elements, all alike. One result is the benefits of being able to enjoy outdoor climate from a private, elevated position right by the harbour. Another is that the shifting of balcony positions means that the view to the sky is unlimited — the upper balcony is not shading the lower.

Individuality and a strong identity are the results on the larger scale. Yet,

the circular floor plate is repeated all the way up, as is the elevator tower and the vertical technical shafts making the construction attractive economically.

At a neighbourhood scale, the circular buildings are placed 'randomly' upon an elevated level. This protective area is softly shaped, has green plants, and provides spaces for outdoor activities like barbecuing and sunbathing, and for children to meet and play.

At an urban scale, circular shaped buildings have no primary direction and therefore integrate more willingly into the rather heterogeneous environment of the former docks with its old industrial buildings, small fishing marinas and, currently, wastelands.

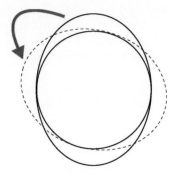

Prefab balconies are mounted
in rotated positions.

The soft shapes allow for
easy passage, little wind
turbulence and views to
all sides.

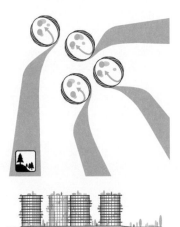

The verdant green is pulled
up and around the facades.

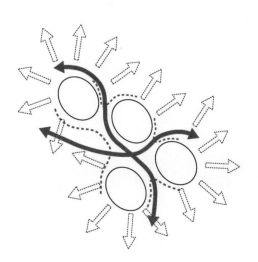

meeting place

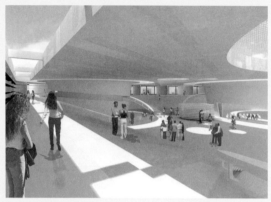

The space between classrooms and plaza is marked by a continuous top light in the roof.

MC *Another aspect of building communities is education and schools. When we discussed schools and education earlier you mentioned the Danish College in Schleswig. What's the main idea behind this school?*

KHN Well it's different to the Ørestad College in functional programme as well as in the layout. It contains a primary and secondary school combined with a college or upper secondary school, preparing students for university, and the main idea was to mix the students around one large space. In this central space there are three big mushroom-shaped elements, each containing a special function: one contains an auditorium, the other facilities for sports, and the third the school library. As far as the classrooms go, they are all around this plaza, where a big staircase connects them. Here again, we tried the idea of the stairs as a meeting place.

MC *Do you think your proposal was more developed or sophisticated in its formal language and approach to education than the other schools in the competition?*

KHN Well the client wrote it off as being too modern, anyway! It was to be located in a new area, where a lot of urban development is going to happen, and one of the qualities I think it had was to be a catalyst. This would have been the first building in this new area, and this building would have embodied that spirit, and become the focal point of the community — like the spark for a new era.

The bowl shaped aula is the natural centre of the Danish College, an education facility for the Danish minority in the northern German region Schleswig.

✳ Danish College in Schleswig

The proposal for the restricted competition for a new Danish College in the German city of Schleswig is compact with a small outer surface. It is designed inside out, but relates to the surroundings as well. The school has six sides directed towards different spaces in the landscape.

A bowl shaped aula is the natural focus of the school and has a knowledge centre and several special facilities. Three round mega-columns embrace the special facilities and define the aula space together with amphi-stairs, well suited for spectators, traffic, leisure and studies. The perimeter encircling the aula is a two-floor reference to the classic English university. Spontaneous meetings and sharing of knowledge has been given flexible opportunities here.

On the other side of the perimeter are the class- and study rooms, focusing on quiet and contemplation. To the outside is yet another perimeter that offers a secondary entrance to the class- and study rooms, and provides the first floor with direct access via outdoor stairs to the surrounding landscape.

The central plaza is open to a wide and flexible variety of uses; educational as well as relaxing. Note the ramp cut into the 'mushroom' to the back — access for all has become an aesthetic addition.

Nieuwegein Stadhuis,
working model.

community centre

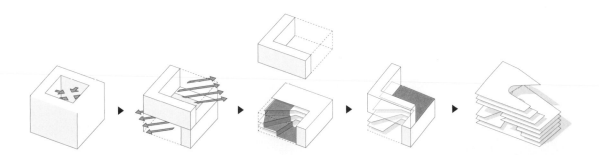

**Transformation from
introvert block to extrovert
terraced structure including
a significant division
between open public levels
and city hall levels.**

MC *Well, we have discussed all kinds of projects and their
roles in the community. The last project I want to talk
about is one that you are developing right now, which is
very interesting for all the aspects it touches upon: the
Stadhuis Nieuwgein — "stadhuis" meaning "city hall"
in Dutch.*

KHN Well, first of all this is very much about building a
new community. It isn't just a town hall but more of a
community centre including a library, a multi-cultural
centre and shops. It is in Nieuwegein, a suburb outside
Utrecht, dating back to the late 1960s. The city is growing
at a very fast pace, but the design of the city centre has
not been very successful. The design and building quality
are poor, and social problems haunt the place. As part of
a regeneration strategy, UN Studio won the competition
for a new masterplan, according to which they are
pulling down major parts of the city centre and building
this town hall as one of two new cornerstones.

MC *With this background I think the project has all the
aspects of building a community. It clearly plays with all
the complexities and interactions that revitalise or keep
a community alive. Tell me about this?*

KHN Well, it was one of those rapid conceptual

competitions where you have a few weeks to come up
with a vision. Looking at the brief, idealistically all the
functions were supposed to be on the ground level, but
obviously this couldn't happen because of the size of
the site. What we did instead was build upon an idea
similar to the one we had used in the Ørestad College;
with differently shaped floor decks where you can
look from one floor to the next; and we placed the
various functions on different levels, but with visual
connections. The town also wanted there to be elevated
gardens, so we designed a garden level that also holds a
restaurant and that is open to the community.

MC *So it does play very much with the community, and,
from what you were telling me, also with the site.*

KHN The site did play into it very much. When we
researched on site, we realised that the building site
presented many different height levels and as you walk
through buildings you can suddenly find yourself on
a different floor. This was obviously a very interesting
aspect that we integrated into the design. Even the
building heights are not uniform; and as a result, those in
our building reflect and play with the surrounding ones.

✳ Stadshuis Nieuwegein

The Stadshuis in Nieuwegein mixes the traditional city hall with a library, a multi-cultural centre, and commercial facilities. In this way, the city hall merges with the every-day world. The design focuses on uniting the wish for intimacy and openness with the desire to envelope an important democratic institution with a certain dignity.

The Stadshuis is designed with terraced open floors that are rotated around a common atrium. The seven levels are connected by an open winding staircase and the rotation of the floor plans allows the visitor a wide view from one floor to the next, all the way up and down through the building. Some of the protruding floors are inter-connected by amphi-staircases that provide for informal rests and rapid internal connections.

The building is an important part of the densification of the city centre and aims to tie the complex context together. Being part of an ambitious city plan, the building is designed with indentations to avoid blocking the daylight, which the neighbouring buildings have previously enjoyed.

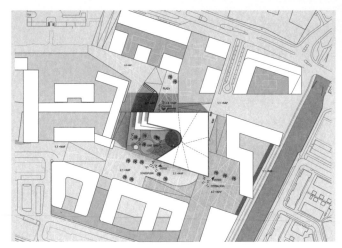

The new city building
(Stadshuis) is to be an
anchor point and
catalyst in the urban
regeneration of an area of
the city developed during
the 1960s.

The terraced floor deck
structure is the basic
architectural expression of
the Stadshuis; outside as
well as on the inside: the
facade is perceived as an
extra skin, draped around
the structure (top), while
inside, the floor decks are
exposed towards the inner
atrium and connected by a
large central staircase.

The facade skin is planned to take on different identities for special occasions using projections or internal lighting features.

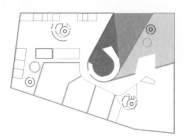

Level 4 I no scale

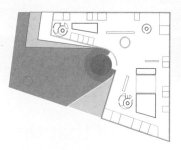

Level 7 I no scale

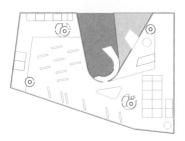

Level 3 I no scale

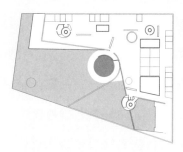

Level 6 I no scale

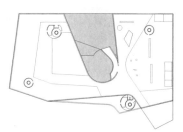

Level 2 I no scale

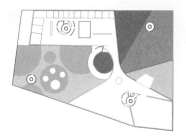

Level 5 I no scale

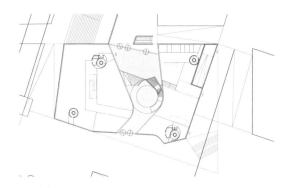

Level 1 I no scale

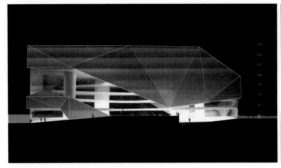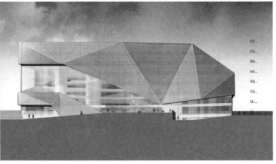

We realised that the building site presented many different height levels and as you walk through buildings you can suddenly find yourself on a different floor. This was obviously a very interesting aspect that we integrated into the design.

MC *Did dialogue with the community also play a key role — did you have time to do this given that it was a competition that you had to respond to very quickly?*
KHN Actually it did, but only after we had won. That's actually when I met Ben van Berkel; as the masterplan architect he was naturally part of the jury for the Stadshuis competition, and at that time we decided that it would be very interesting to collaborate. After the competition, that's when the dialogue really started, both with the city planners, the masterplan architects and with the many users of the building. We had a lot of workshops with the users, because this was essential in achieving the goals for this new building; to create a new positive spirit in the community and for everyone to feel that this was to become their house. So the workshops went on with four different groups, each consisting of related users or subjects. For instance, one group was about technical, security and automation, another was all about the city hall functions, while a third dealt with all the local community users. The idea was to have everyone experience that mutual compromises were necessary to make this complex logistic work with benefit for all, and to create an obligating ownership for the solutions that were worked out by all, in partnership. In the workshops with the city planners and with Ben we wanted to get across to them that it was very much about movement and connections; to realise the story of how to connect the new town.
MC *Looking at the images the other thing that seems to be different is the facade; here [in these images] it looks simpler but I believe there is an idea behind it.*
KHN The idea was to have a fairly simple and basic facade system since the budget was low. However, it has a kind of pattern and that's again where the research department kicks in. They are researching a material that can either be used or incorporated in the facade. We want to weave into the facade a kind of textile that can play with different densities. We are always experimenting and trying to find new solutions, and this is one of the examples.

An elevated roof garden marks the city hall position in the mixed-use building.

MC *So where do you see your architecture for the future?*
KHN When I try to look forward in the years to come,
I think our development can be compared to a tree.
We've grown with a constant firm core — the trunk,
and now it's going to be more and more dynamic; we
will explore more and more diverse branches. They
will move in new directions, but remain connected to
the trunk, at least as a starting point. Our new projects
will, in other words, stand on the shoulders of those
that went before, but they must also explore new
frontiers. We are still playing a lot with stories and we
will continue to do so, but the idea is that it will always
depend on the task and what we are trying to achieve.
It's what the brief requires, not just one specific
signature architecture. In addition to that, I expect a
lot from our research department, and the fact that we
have enlarged our circle of owners with three young
and talented architects. All three lead our competition
and development units and contribute significantly to
the internal debates, investigations and explorations.

MC *How would you like to be remembered, or rather,
what would you like to be remembered for, as
contributing to the architectural world?*
KHN That's a big question! Maybe as a storyteller, like
Karen Blixen.... For me it isn't just about the process
and the approach, it's about the idea and what actually
stands at the end. I think that what is important is
to have created architecture that influences human
behaviour; enhances interaction and positive meetings
between people. Like for example the Ørestad College.
I hope that this building will create a new way of
teaching and learning. So to sum it up, I would like
to be remembered for having the ability to change
people's way of behaving and their approach to life.

Zooming out, I would be satisfied if people see our
achievements as the silhouette of the tree I spoke of
before, and that they will find that all the different
branches, however bent or strangely shaped they may
seem alone, together form a beautiful, perfect crown
like that of an old solitary oak tree....

Biographies

Kim Herforth Nielsen

Kim Herforth Nielsen was born in 1954 and raised in Denmark. Graduating in 1981 from the Århus School of Architecture AAA, Kim works at CF Møller Architects until 1986 where he founds his studio named Nielsen, Nielsen & Nielsen together with two study companions. The studio's name is changed in 1995 to 3XNielsen.

3XN has reached an international level over a period of relatively few years. In 1999, 3XN finished the Royal Danish Embassy in Berlin; the first building for 3XN outside Denmark. The Berlin Embassy led to an invitation for the international competition for the new Music Building for Amsterdam, The Netherlands; inaugurated in 2005 the project boosted international attention to 3XN. Participation in international competitions grew and today, more than 50 per cent of 3XN's work is outside Denmark.

Kim Herforth Nielsen is concurrently investing much time in lecturing around the world, especially in universities, schools of architecture and related institutions, but also in significant business forums. Kim received the Eckersberg Médaille, awarded for artists of highest performance in Denmark, and was later awarded, by the Queen of Denmark, the distinguished Knight's Cross with the right to carry Dannebrog.

Kim is a chartered member of the RIBA. On two occasions, 3XN's work was honoured with an RIBA European Award; the latest for Alsion University, 2007. With 3XN, Kim exhibits works worldwide, including at the 9th International Architecture Exhibition la Biennale di Venezia, METAMORPH, where he meets Matteo Cainer. Kim Herforth Nielsen serves, on a regular basis, as judge in Danish AA competitions, and served in the AR40 jury in the UK.

Since 2004, Kim Herforth Nielsen remains the sole founder of 3XN, the final abbreviated name for the practice. The office has now six Partners. It has expanded out of its Århus base and now has its head office in Copenhagen. Today, the two offices comprise a little over 100 architects and other employees.

Kim moved himself and his family to the Danish capital in 2006 so as to be able to oversee the rapid growth of the new head office, and to benefit from international flight connections from Copenhagen airport to the rest of the world.

Matteo Cainer

Born to Italian parents in Canada in 1972, Matteo Cainer spends most of his early years between Egypt, the United States and Italy. After receiving his architectural degree from the University of Architecture in Venice, he moves for a short period to Milano.

In 1999 he moves to New York City to work for Peter Eisenman. During this time he works on international competitions and a variety of projects both as design and project architect. The City of Culture of Galicia and the Arizona Stadium are among a few of the projects together with the Berlin Holocaust Memorial, inaugurated in 2005. In 2003 he moves to Austria to work for the Vienna based firm Coop Himmelblau. Here he works on projects like the Akron Art Museum and the BMW Welt project in Munich.

In 2004 Matteo is offered the position of Assistant Director to Kurt W Forster, for the 9th International Architecture Exhibition la Biennale di Venezia, METAMORPH. On this occasion his role is not only as assistant curator but as coordinator of exhibition design, as well as liaison to the architecture studios.

In 2005 he returns to Milan, where he collaborates briefly with the Japanese studio of Arata Isozaki Associates working on the City Life project. In the last months of 2005 he moves to London, here his involvements are in multiple fields, both working for Fletcher Priest Architects on projects like Stratford City, and as visiting critic at the Bartlett School of Architecture, Pratt Architecture School and Columbia University in New York.

Project credits

Museum of Liverpool

Address: Mann Island, Liverpool, UK **Client:** National Museums Liverpool **Gross floor area:** 13,000 m² Competition: 2004 Completion: 2005–2010 **3XN team:** Kim Herforth Nielsen, Kim Christiansen, Bo Boje Larsen, Thomas Käszner, Michael Kruse, Per Damgaard-Sørensen, Martin Musiatowicz, Melanie Zirn, Trine Dalgaard, Malene Knudsen, Thomas Kranz, Jørgen Søndermark, Rikke Zachariasen, Pia Hallstrup, Anne-Mette Hansen, Heidi Daggry, Helge Arno, Carsten Olsen, Dan Hinge, Dan Thirstrup, Erik Frehr Hansen, Marianne Els, Jacob G Nielsen, Morten Mygind, Christian Engbirk, Mogens Brun Jepsen, Klaus Purup **Engineer:** Buro Happold, UK Engineer: Buro Happold **Landscape archtitects:** Schønherr Landskab

Herning House of Art

Address: Birk Centerpark, Herning, DK **Client:** Herning House of Art Foundation **Competition:** 2005 **Gross floor area:** 4,800 m2 **3XN team:** Kim Herforth Nielsen, Jan Ammundsen, Tommy Bruun, Flemming Tanghus, Martin Krogh Hansen, Jørgen Søndermark, Rikke Zachariasen, Heidi Daggry **Renderings:** 3XN and Uniform **Engineer:** Rambøll A/S **Acoustics:** Peutz bv

The Lighthouse

Address: Århus Harbourfront **Architects:** 3XN and UN Studio **Urban Environment Design:** Gehl Architects **Light House Consortium:** Keops Development, Frederiksbjerg Ejendomme, Arbejdernes Andels Boligforening, Boligforeningen Ringgaarden **Gross floor area:** 58,000 floor meters **Competition:** 2007 **Completion:** 2011 **3XN team:** Kim Herforth Nielsen, Bodil Nordstrøm, Børge Motland, Christina Melholt Brogaard, Jørgen Søndermark, Kim Christiansen, Klaus Mikkelsen, Michael Kruse, Per Damgaard-Sørensen, Rikke Sørensen , Rikke Zachariasen, Rune Bjerno Nielsen, Stefan Nors Jensen — model, Stine Hviid Jensen, Thomas Meldgaard Pedersen, Tommy Bruun, Palle Holsting, Lone Bak, Jørn Juul Sørensen, Lars Kjemtrup, Steen Blach Petersen, Stefan Nors Jensen, Mads Agger, Trine Dalgaard, Marianne Els, Pia Timm Hagmann **UN Studio team:** Ben van Berkel, Caroline Bos with Christian Veddeler, Astrid Piber and Juliane Maier, Michael Knauss, Morten Krog, Markus van Aalderen, Steffen Riegas, Juliane Maier **Gehl team:** Jan Gehl, Helle Søholt, Ewa Westermark, Kristian S. Villadsen

Kristiansand Theatre and Music Centre

Address: Silokai, Kristiansand, NO **Client:** Kristiansand Bystyre, Vest-Agder Fylkesting **Gross floor area:** 16,000 m² **3XN team:** Kim Herforth Nielsen, Michael Kruse, Tommy Bruun, Per Damgaard-Sørensen, Mette Baarup, Lars Gylling, Martin Musiatowicz, Melanie Zirn, Jørgen Søndermark, Rikke Zachariasen, Maj Quist **Engineer:** Arup Acoustics, UK

Ørestad College

Address: Ørestad Boulevard/Arne Jacobsens Allé, Copenhagen, DK **Client:** Municipality of Copenhagen **Gross floor area:** 12,000 m² **Competition:** 2003 **Completion:** 2004–2007 **3XN team:** Kim Herforth Nielsen, Michael Kruse, Tommy Bruun, Per Damgaard-Sørensen, Trine Berthold, Kristjan Eggertsson, Jørgen Søndermark, Rikke Zachariasen, Pia Hallstrup, Maj Quist, Rasmus Kruse, Lars Ketil Carlsen, Anders Barslund Christensen, Morten Mygind, Nicolaj Borgwardt Schmidt, Trine Dalgaard, Britt Hansen, Ritha Jørgensen, Flemming Vind Christiansen, Holger Mouritzen, Klaus Mikkelsen, Robin Vind Christiansen, Klaus Petersen, Allan Brinch, Mogens Jepsen, Palle Holsting **Engineer:** Søren Jensen A/S **Adviser:** Cand. pæd. ph.d Helle Mathiasen

Lisbjerg School

Address: Lisbjerg, Århus, DK **Client:** Municipaity of Århus **Competition:** 2006 **3XN team:** Kim Herforth Nielsen, Tommy Bruun, Rasmus Kruse, Flemming Tanghus, Rune Bjerno Nielsen, Jørgen Søndermark, Daniel De Sousa, Bodil Nordstrøm, Heidi Daggry, Christina Melholt Brogaard

Yangpu Gateway Buildings

Address: Song Hu Road, Shanghai, China **Client:** Shui On Land Development **Gross floor area:** 30,000 m² **Competition:** 2004 **3XN team:** Kim Herforth Nielsen, Bo Boje Larsen, Tommy Bruun, Rasmus Kruse, Lars Ketil Carlsen, Martin Musiatowicz, Junliang Lu, Heidi Daggry

Saxo Bank

Address: Philip Heymans Allé, 2900 Hellerup, DK **Client:** Saxo Bank/Carlsberg Properties **Gross floor area:** 16,000m² **Competion:** 2004 **Completion:** 2004–2008 **3XN team:** Kim Herforth Nielsen, Bo Boje Larsen, Klaus Mikkelsen, Flemming Tanghus, Mette Baarup, Anne Strandgaard Hansen, Jakob Ohm Laursen, Torsten Wang, Olaf Kunert, Esther Clemmensen, Rikke Rützou Arnved, Esben Trier Nielsen, Melanie Zirn, Rasmus Kruse, Jan Ammundsen, Helge Skovsted, Robin Vind Christiansen, Jesper Malmkjær, Jeanette Hansen **Engineer:** Rambøll A/S **Contractor:** KPC Byg A/S

Renault Truckland

Client: Classified **Gross floor area:** 21,000 m² **3XN team:** Kim Herforth Nielsen, Jan Ammundsen, Rasmus Kruse Jensen, Tommy Bruun, Lars Ketil Carlsen, Robert Haff-Jensen, Bjarne Korsgaard, Jørgen Søndermark, Rikke Zachariasen, Heidi Daggry, Henrik Bisp **Engineer:** ARUP, GEC Ingénierie **Landscape:** Schønherr Landskab

The Museum of Modern Art in Warsaw

Address: Warsaw, Poland **Client:** Municipality of Warsaw **Gross floor area:** 35,000 m² **Competition:** 2007 **3XN team:** Kim Herforth Nielsen, Tommy Bruun, Rune Bjerno Nielsen, Flemming Tanghus, Christina Melholt Brogaard, Rikke Zachariasen, Jørgen Søndermark **Language Advisor:** Andrzej Morks

The Royal Danish Embassy

Address: The Nordic Embassy Complex, Berlin Tiergaten, DE **Client:** The Danish Ministry of Foreign Affairs **Competition:** 1996 **Gross floor area:** 2,650 m² **Completion:** 1997–1999 **3XN team:** Kim Herforth Nielsen, Lars Frank Nielsen, Gerti Axelsen, Lars Kjemtrup, Jørgen Søndermark, Lars Due Jensen, Jette Schwarz von Oettingen, Helge Skovsted, Lars Povlsen, Mads Posch, Malene E Knudsen **Engineer, Technics:** IGH Köln **Engineer, Statistics:** IGH Berlin **Contractor:** NCC **Photo:** Finn Christoffersen

Bella Hotels

Address: Bella Centre, Centre Boulevard 5, Copenhagen, DK **Client:** Copenhagen Congress Centre/Bella Centre **Gross floor area:** 31,000 m² in total, Phase 1 16,000 m², Phase 2 15,000 m² **Rooms:** 800, 400 in each tower **Competition:** 2007 **3XN team** Kim Herforth Nielsen, Bo Boje Larsen, Jan Ammundsen, Marie Hesseldahl Larsen, Maiken Schmidt Nielsen, Børge Motland, Svend Roald Jensen, Jørgen Søndermark, Bodil Nordstrøm, Anne Strandgaard Hansen, Jesper Malmkjær, Turid Ohlsson, Thomas Bang Jespersen, Martin Reinholdt Frederiksen, Mads Leth Jensen, Esther Clemmensen, Anders Bak, Helle Vestergaard **Engineer:** Rambøll A/S

Alsion

Address: Alsion 2 , Sønderborg, DK **Client:** Danish University and Property Agency + Science Park of Southern Denmark A/S + Sønderborg Foundation Concert Hall + Sønderborg municipality **Gross floor area:** 28,500 m² **Competition:** 2002 **Completion:** 2007 **Award:** RIBA European Award 2007 **3XN team:** Kim Herforth Nielsen, Anne Mikkelsen, Rasmus Holm, Egon Jacobsen, Carsten Olsen, Christian Bolding, Lars Povlsen, Lars Kjemtrup, Mette Baarup, Lars Gylling, Michael Kruse, Kim Christiansen, Allan Edmund Hansen, Christian Dahl, Anders Barslund Christensen, Morten Kramer, Morten Sjørvad, Nicolaj Borgwardt Schmidt, Ritha Jørgensen, Malene Knudsen, Hanne Højgaard Sørensen, Holger Mouritzen, Jeanette Due Andersen, Lars Serup, Ingvar Stefansson, Thomas Pedersen, Jens Knudsen, Jørgen Søndermark, Pia Hallstrup, Rikke Zachariasen, Maj Quist **Engineer:** Strunge & Hartvigsen with Buro Happold, Consulting Engineers **Engineer acoustics:** Arup Acoustics **Architect Landscape:** Schønherr Landskab **Photo:** Adam Mørk

Middelfart Savings Bank
Address: Algade, Middelfart, DK Client: Trekantens Ejendomsselskab A/S Award: Mipin AR Future Awards 2006; "Officies" Gross floor area: 5,000 m² Competition: 2005 Completion: 2008 3XN team: Kim Herforth Nielsen, Klaus Mikkelsen, Jens Henrik S Birkmose, Rasmus Kruse Jensen, Helge Skovsted, Flemming Tanghus, Tommy Ladegaard, Peder Kragelund, Jan Ammundsen, Morten Mygind, Tommy Bruun, Jørgen Søndermark, Rikke Zachariasen, Heidi Daggry, Johanne Holmsberg, Stefan Nors. Engineer: COWI Architect Landscape: Schønherr Landskab

Kronjylland Savings Bank
Address: Tronholmen, Randers, DK Client: Kronjylland Savings Bank Gross floor area: 7,600 m² Competition: 1999 Completion: 2002 3XN team: Kim Herforth Nielsen, Mette Dalsgaard, Gerti Axelsen, Lars Povlsen, Lars Due Jensen, Tommy Bruun, Klaus Petersen, Anders Barslund Christensen, Jørgen Søndermark, Rikke Zachariasen, Pia Hallstrup, Flemming Vind Christiansen, Holger Mouritzen, Rasmus Holscher Architect Landscape: Kristine Jensen Art Wall: Jens Bjerre Engineer: Rambøll A/S Contractor: NCC

Deloitte Headquarters
Address: Weidekampsgade 6, Copenhagen, DK Client: Deloitte Gross floor area: 26,000 m² + basement 12,000 m² Completion: 2005 3XN team: Kim Herforth Nielsen, Torben Østergaard, Per Damgaard-Sørensen, Helge Skovsted, Morten Mygind, Thomas Kranz, Poul Jørgensen, Eva Hard, Heidi Sørensen, Anders Holm, Trine Berthold, Morten Kramer, Ole Østergaard, Jørgen Søndermark, Rikke Zachariasen, Pia Hallstrup, Maj Quist Client advisor: Iver Albæk Byggerådgivning Landscape architect: Jeppe Aagaard Andersen Interior consultants: Signal Arkitekter Light artist : Steven Scott Consulting engineers: Leif Hansen Rådgivende Ingeniører FRI Main contractor: KPC BYG A/S Photo: Adam Mørk

Tivoli Concert Hall Pavilion
Address: Tivoli, Vesterbrogade 3, Copenhagen, DK Client: Tivoli Gross floor area: Existing area 10,000 m² + new build area 4,000 m² Completion: 2005 3XN team: Kim Herforth Nielsen, Bo Boje Larsen, Anne Strandgaard Hansen, Julie Daugaard Jensen, Jakob Ohm Laursen, Jeanette Hansen, Kasper Hertz, Christine Pedersen, Esther Clemmensen, Teddy Pelle-Olsen, Anja Pedersen Engineer: Arup, Birch & Krogboe Contractor: NCC Photo: Adam Mørk

Am Kaffeelager
Address: Lehrter Stadtquartier, Berlin Client: Vivico Real Estate GmbH Gross floor area: 21,000 m² Competition: 2004 3XN team: Kim Herforth Nielsen, Michael Kruse, Tommy Bruun, Lars Kjemtrup, Thomas Pedersen, Rune Bjerno Nielsen, Børge Motland, Maiken Shcmidt Nielsen, Henriette Byrge, Jørgen Søndermark, Bodil Nordstrøm, Christina Melholt Brogaard Engineer: Buro Happold, Berlin Local architect: Architekten QBQ

Het Muziekgebouw
Address: Piet HeinKade 1, Amsterdam, NL Client: Municipality of Amsterdam Awards: Dutch Building Award 2006 (Nederlandse Bouwprijs 2006, best Dutch building 2006), ULI Award Europe 2006 Dedalo-Minosse Special Prize 2006, LEAF Award 2006 Gross floor area: 15,000 m² Competition: 1997 Completion: 2005 3XN team: Kim Herforth Nielsen, Palle Holsting, Rasmus Holm, Torben Østergaard, Ole Østergaard, Uffe Bay-Schmidt, Flemming Vind Christiansen, Eva Hard, Troels Chresten Højlund, Poul Jørgensen, Ingvar Stefanss, Jette Oettingen, Jørgen Søndermark, Rikke Zachariasen, Pia Hallstrup Project architecs: 3XN, Århus, Denmark and ABT-bouwkunde, The Netherlands Project manager: ABT-pm, The Netherlands Interior architect: 3XN in general; 3XN & Christian Bauma (BIMhuis) Artist: Assisting light artist Steeven Scott, Denmark. Structural Engineer: ABT BV, The Netherlands Engineer HVAC: Royal Haskoning, The Netherlands Acoustics enginner: Peutz BV, The Netherlands Contractor: BAM, the Netherlands Installations contractor: ULC Group, The Netherlands Theatre consultant: Hans Wolff & Partners BV, The Netherlands

Rainbow project
Address: Dublin, Ireland Gross floor area: 186,000 m² Competition: 2006 3XN team: Kim Herforth Nielsen, Jan Ammundsen, Marie Hesseldahl, Lars Kjemtrup, Rasmus Kruse, Jørgen Søndermark, Bodil Nordstrøm, Rikke Zachariasen, Tommy Bruun, Christina Melholt Brogaard

Nordhavnen Residences
Address: Nordhavnen, Copenhagen DK Client: SQ Gross floor area: 20,000 m² Competition: 2004 3XN team: Kim Herforth Nielsen, Henriette Byrge, Melanie Zirn, Jan Ammundsen Award: Mipin AR Project Award 2006; "Residential"

Danish College in Schleswig
Address: Slesvig, DK Client: Municipality of Slesvi Gross floor area: 14.000 m2 Competition: 2006 3XN team: Kim Herforth Nielsen, Tommy Bruun, Jan Ammundsen, Flemming Tanghus, Rasmus Kruse, Stig Hesselund, Jørgen Søndermark, Rikke Zachariasen

Stadshuis Nieuwegein
Address: Nieuwegein, Utrecht, NL DK Client: Nieuwegein Municipality Gross floor area: 25.000 m2 Competition: 2006 3XN team: Kim Herforth Nielsen, Mette Baarup, Henriette Byrge, Daniel de Sousa, Robert Haff-Jensen, Palle Holsting, Jørgen Søndermark, Heidi Daggry, Rune Hvarre Brouer, Nicolaj Borgwardt Schmidt, Vibeke Jørensen

3XN partners

Kim Herforth Nielsen   Kim Christiansen   Bo Boje Larsen   Michael Kruse   Jan Ammundsen   Tommy Bruun

Kim Herforth Nielsen

Kim Herforth Nielsen, founder of 3XN, is Principal Architect. Kim Herforth Nielsen holds full architectural responsibility for all 3XN products from original concept to turnkey building. Kim is physically present at 3XN's two offices in Denmark on an equal base in order to maintain a strong sense of idea and the highest quality in all projects that leave the desks at 3XN.

Kim has been a main driving force in 3XN's 20 years of history, with projects like the Royal Danish Embassy in Berlin. Kim was honoured with the Danish Knight's Cross, he is judge in the Danish Architectural Association's competitions, sits in the AR Emerging Architects Award jury and is a frequent lecturer at architects' schools, universities, and business forums.

Kim Christiansen

Kim Christiansen is CEO, Partner since 2000. Architect at 3XN since 1994. Kim Christiansen is responsible for all economical and contractual relationships with clients and cooperating partners.

Internally, Kim holds overall responsibility for projecting, documentation and quality assurance as well as planning and Human Resources. Kim Christiansen is based in the Århus office.

Bo Boje Larsen

Bo Boje Larsen is Managing Director with main responsibility for strategy, organisation and the Copenhagen office. Bo Boje Larsen joined as Partner at 3XN in 2003 after ten years of management at the Henning Larsens Tegnestue. Of these he worked the last seven years as Chief Architect and Managing Director.

Bo has worked with all aspects of the architectural business; competitions, preliminary sketching, projecting, documentation, supervision, construction management, project management — including such very large projects such as the Copenhagen Opera.

Michael Kruse

Born in 1970, Michael Kruse was educated at the Århus School of Architecture. Michael came to 3XN in 2002 from a position at David Chipperfield's studio, and is Partner in 3XN since 2007. He heads the Århus Competition Department, together with Tommy Bruun. His experience encompasses major projects such as Lighthouse (1st prize), Museum of Liverpool (1st prize), Kunshan masterplan (1st prize) and Ørestad College (1st prize).

Jan Ammundsen

Jan Ammundsen was born in 1972 and educated at the Århus School of Architecture. He is a Partner at 3XN since 2007.

Jan came to 3XN in 2005, where he headed the Competition Department in the Århus office, with major 1st prize competitions like Middelfart Savings Bank and the Stadium of Horsens. He then transferred to the Copenhagen office to develop the Competition Department there to the same high level as that at Århus, with major successes like the Bella Hotels, the Rainbow project (2nd prize) and BARCODE residences (1st prize).

Tommy Bruun

Tommy Brunn was born in 1971 and educated at the Århus School of Architecture. Tommy came to 3XN 1999, and is Partner in 3XN since 2007.

He heads the Århus Competition Department, together with Michael Kruse. His major work includes the Warsaw Museum of Modern Art, Herning House of Art, Yangpu Gateway and Ørestad College in Copenhagen (1st prize).

Realised projects 1988 – present

1988
Blangstedgaard, Residences
5 PKA Pensionskasser, Residential,
20 apartments, 44 – 110 m2, Odense, Denmark

Villa Fire
Hanne and Jørgen Malmberg, Single family
house
166 m², Århus, Denmark

1991
Culture and Congress Centre, Holstebro
Municipality of Holstebro, Culture,
13,500 m², Holstebro, Denmark

1992
Holstebro Court Building
The Danish Ministry of Justice, Public,
1,000 m², Holstebro, Denmark

Emiliedalen
PFA Byg A/S, Residential,
340 apartments, Århus, Denmark

1993
Hinnerup Library
Municipality of Hinnerup, Public/Culture,
1,700 m², Hinnerup, Denmark

Hinnerup Swimming Bath
Municipality of Hinnerup, Public/Culture,
2,000 m², Hinnerup, Denmark

DGI Headquarters
Danske Gymnastik-og Idrætsforeninger,
Business,
2,300 m², Vejle, Denmark

1995
Dalum Polytechnic
The Danish Ministry of Education, Education,
2,300 m², Odense, Denmark

1996
Architects Building
Architects' Pension Fund, Business,
3,500 m², Copenhagen, Denmark

Villa Vadstrup
Wibeke and Steen Vadstrup, Single family
house,
156 m², Slagelse, Denmark

1997
Dalum Polytechnic, The main entrance
The Danish Ministry of Education, Education,
300 m², Odense, Denmark

**Datagraf — Design and Administration
Company**
Datagraf Properties A/S, Office,
3,000 m², Auning, Denmark

Film Centre, Gutenberghouse
The Danish Ministry of Culture, Culture,
3,000 m², Copenhagen, Denmark

Grindsted Business School
The Danish Ministry of Education, Education,
225 m², Grindsted, Denmark

Roskilde Hall
Roskilde Hallen amba, Public,
10,000 m², Roskilde, Denmark

Aalborg Polytechnic
Aalborg Polytechnic, Education,
5,000 m², Aalborg, Denmark

1998
Blaagaard Teachers College
The Danish Ministry of Education, Education,
3,800 m², Søborg, Denmark

Norra Hammen
Riksbyggen Norra Skåne, Residential,
55 apartments, Helsingborg, Sweden

Oceanarium
Municipality of Hirtshals, Culture,
5,000 m², Hirtshals, Denmark

Rambøll Headquarters
Danica Pension Ejendomsinvest, Office,
6,800 m², Århus, Denmark

Eco-House "99"
AAB Kolding, Housing,
5,100 m², Kolding, Denmark

Langager School
Municipality of Århus, Education,
4,600 m², Århus, Denmark

1999
ATP Domicile
ATP Properties, Office,
4,450 m², Hillerød, Denmark

The Royal Danish Embassy
The Danish Ministry of Foreign Affairs, Public,
2,650 m², Berlin, Germany

2000
SID Domicile
SID Århus, Office,
2,600 m², Århus, Denmark

Department of Social and Health Services
Municipality of Århus, Public,
14,000 m², Århus, Denmark

World On-line, Domicile
World On-line, Business,
12,000 m², Copenhagen, Denmark

2001
Tactical Air Command
Ministry of Defence, Building Service, Public,
5,600 m², Karup, Denmark

Siemens Mobile Phones
PFA, Office,
17,000 m², Nørresundby, Denmark

Smedegade Senior Care Centre
KAB, Residential,
6,750 m², Slagelse, Denmark

2002
America Pier Residences
Nordea Properties A/S, Residential,
9,700 m², Copenhagen, Denmark

FIH Domicile
FIH, Business,
12,000 m², Copenhagen, Denmark

Kronjyllands Savings Bank
Kronjylland Savings Bank, Business,
7,600 m², Randers, Denmark

**Exhibition at The National Museum,
"The Spirit of Nature"**
Danish National Museum, Culture, Egmont Hall,
1,000 m², Copenhagen, Denmark

Filosofparken
ABF of 1899, Residential,
9,000 m², Roskilde, Denmark

2003
Nesselande
Municipality of Rotterdam, Business,
25,000 m², Rotterdam, Netherlands

Sampension Headquarters
Sampension, Business,
9,500 m², Hellerup, Denmark

DGI Urban Sports Centre
Den Selvejende Institution DGI Huset, Culture,
4,500 m², Århus, Denmark

2004
Bruuns Galleri Shopping Centre (with SHL)
NCC and Steen & Strøm A/S, Culture / Public,
66,000 m², Århus, Denmark

Dalby School
Municipality of Kolding, Education,
2,600 m², Kolding, Denmark

Senior Care Residences, Bramdrup
Municipality of Kolding, Residential,
5,500 m², Kolding, Denmark

DFDS Terminal
Copenhagen Harbour A/S and CMP, Office,
5,300 m², Copenhagen, Denmark

2005
Het Muziekgebouw/BIMHUIS
Amsterdam Municipality, Culture,
13,400 m², Amsterdam, The Netherlands

Deloitte Building
Deloitte, Business,
26,000 m², Copenhagen, Denmark

M2 Houses — Ongoing
M2, Residential,
150–200 m², Denmark

**Exhibition at The National Museum,
"The Curfew"**
Danish National Museum, Culture,
Egmont Hall, 1,000 m², Copenhagen, Denmark

Tivoli Concert Hall and Pavilion
Tivoli, Culture,
4,000 m², Copenhagen, Denmark

2006
Almere Buiten
Multi Vastegoed bv, Residential and office,
29,000 m², Almere Buiten, The Netherlands

Glass Museum, Ebeltoft
Glasmuseet Ebeltoft, Culture,
2,500 m², Ebeltoft, Denmark

Teaching Faculty, University of Gothenburg
Gothenburg University, Education,
12,500 m², Göteborg, Sweden

2007
Vousaari Tower
Paulig Ltd, Residential,
6,600 m², Helsinki, Finland

Ørestad College
Municipality of Copenhagen, Education,
12,000 m², Copenhagen, Denmark

**Alsion University,
Concert Hall and Science Park**
Danish State's Research and Education
Buildings + Science Park South A/S, Education,
28,500 m², Sønderborg, Denmark

2008
Bryggen Shopping Mall
(with SHL)
Steen & Strøm A/S, Culture / Public,
50,000 m², Vejle, Denmark

"City of all ages"
Copenhagen Municipality, Dwellings,
15,000 m², Valby, Denmark

Horsens Stadium
Horsens Municipality, Culture,
6,500 m², 10,000 seats (football), 30,000 people
(concerts), Horsens, Denmark

Middelfart Savings Bank
Trekantens Ejendomsselskab A/S, Office,
5,000 m², Middelfart, Denmark

Ørestad City Residences
AB+FB/KSB, Residential,
12,000 m², Copenhagen, Denmark

Saxo Bank
Carsberg Properties, Office,
22,500 m², Hellerup, Denmark

2009
Tangen VGS, Kristiansand
Vest Agder Fylkeskommune, Education,
17,300 m², Kristiansand, Norway

Bella Center Hotels
Copenhagen Congress Center / Bella Center,
Culture/Public

31,000 m², Copenhagen, Denmark

2010
Museum of Liverpool
National Museums Liverpool, Culture,
13,000 m², Liverpool, United Kingdom

Stadshuis Nieuwegein
Nieuwegein Municipality, Public,
25,000 m², Utrecht, The Netherlands

Wide Planet Resort
Dromaco, Turkey, Residential,
150,000 m², Candarli, Turkey

2011
Lighthouse
(With UN Studio and Gehl Architects)
Municipality of Aarhus, Culture/Public/
Residential,
63,000 m², Århus, Denmark

2014
Barcode Residences
OSU Oslo S Utvikling A/S, Residential/Culture/
Office, 13,000 m²–45,000 m², Oslo, Norway

preface
Paul Finch

introduction
Kent Martinussen

interview
Matteo Cainer

project texts and captions
Jørgen Søndermark

editing
Jørgen Søndermark
Matteo Cainer

graphic design
Bodil Nordstrøm
Karen Willcox

graphic design assistants
Rikke Zachariasen
Christina Brogaard

architecture art design
fashion history photography
theory and things

black dog
publishing

www.blackdogonline.com london uk

© 2007 Black Dog Publishing Limited, London, UK
and the authors
All rights reserved

Black Dog Publishing Limited
10A Acton Street
London
WC1X 9NG
UK

British Library Cataloguing-in-Publication Data.
A CIP record for this book is available from
the British Library.
ISBN 978 1 906155 23 0

Black Dog Publishing Limited, London, UK, is an
environmentally responsible company.